The Joint Military Intelligence College supports and encourages research on intelligence issues that distills lessons and improves Intelligence Community capabilities for policy-level and operational consumers

This series of Discussion Papers presents the work of faculty, students and others whose research on intelligence issues is supported or otherwise encouraged by the Joint Military Intelligence College (JMIC) through its Center for Strategic Intelligence Research. Discussion Papers are distributed to Department of Defense schools and to the Intelligence Community, and unclassified papers are available to the public through the National Technical Information Service (*www.ntis.gov*).

This paper is the product of research undertaken throughout Fiscal Year 2003 by a senior Research Fellow with the College's Center for Strategic Intelligence Research. This paper, like others in the series, has been reviewed by senior experts from across the Intelligence Community. The comments of one of those reviewers are included to highlight differing perspectives on the issues raised by the author.

This publication has been approved for unrestricted distribution by the Directorate for Freedom of Information and Security Review, Washington Headquarters Services.

Russell.Swenson@dia.mil, **Editor and Director**
Center for Strategic Intelligence Research

Discussion Paper Number Thirteen

GLOBAL WAR ON TERRORISM: ANALYZING THE STRATEGIC THREAT

WASHINGTON, DC
November 2004

CONTENTS

GLOBAL WAR ON TERRORISM: ANALYZING THE STRATEGIC THREAT

Editor's Preface

The establishment of the Center for Strategic Intelligence Research (CSIR) at the Joint Military Intelligence College (JMIC) has allowed for Intelligence Community (IC) professionals, who participate with the Center as Research Fellows, to blend their unique talents with those of academia. This has resulted in the publication of several books and papers since 2003 that bring these two approaches together. A result of this CSIR process is presented in this paper, which was researched and written by a senior Research Fellow from October 2002 to September 2003. The work is not meant to be an end point in the dialog between intelligence and academia, but only a start toward invigorating the debate as to how best to focus IC energies and resources to engage in what is currently being called the "Global War On Terrorism" (GWOT).

The IC mission is to organize itself and educate or train its analysts in such a way as to create the capability for accurately informing both policymakers and warfighters. In the "GWOT," the United States faces a type of war that is unique in its history. The IC must accept the responsibility for defining that war by providing an understanding of the enemy, his strengths, weaknesses, and worldview. It is only with this understanding that U.S. policymakers can begin to define victory, and articulate the ramifications of defeat. U.S. forces and IC assets must also adapt to what will likely be a prolonged conflict by modifying structures, equipment, and intelligence collection capabilities to counter the strategic, operational, and tactical threat—threats that the IC must understand and define and for which it must establish intelligence collection requirements. The global Jihad being waged against the United States is not a matter for an "intelligence task force," but rather for an entire mobilized and focused IC, acting with anticipatory engagement over a prolonged period. Intelligence analysts entering the Community today should be prepared for the "counter-Jihad" to define their careers, just as the Cold War defined the careers of their predecessors. Any lesser effort on the part of the IC will be insufficient. Things that are "too hard to do" must be defined and accomplished.

The strength of the Center for Strategic Intelligence Research is in providing an environment that uniquely blends intelligence analysis and academic freedom to generate new, and rightly controversial, syntheses. The result of any ensuing debates, as suggested by the author, should be an Intelligence Community optimally staffed and organized to help lead this nation toward an effective counter-Jihad in the "Global War on Terrorism." The editor hopes that this publication will broaden ongoing debate over the role of government in prosecuting this world-wide conflict.

A Commentary on

GLOBAL WAR ON TERRORISM: ANALYZING THE STRATEGIC THREAT

Max L. Gross[1]

Since the infamous attacks on the United States of 11 September 2001, there has been a tendency in some quarters to lay the blame on Islam. Others, not wanting to go so far, have pointed the finger of guilt at Wahhabism, a particular school of thought within the Islamic world most closely associated with the Kingdom of Saudi Arabia. Still others, wary of indicting a whole religion, the heart-felt belief system of approximately one-fifth of humanity, have argued that the al-Qa'ida movement of Osama bin Laden and others, that most believe was responsible for the 9/11 attacks, has been engaged in an effort to "hijack" Islam. Within the Islamic world itself, those who have sought to dissociate "mainstream" Islam from the al-Qa'ida jihadists have tended to label them *khawarij* (seceeders), a term that hearkens back to the early days of Islam, when a group of early Muslims, disillusioned with the Sunni-Shia split over who should lead the new political-religious Islamic movement, "seceded" from the larger community and went their own way. Notably, the early *khawarij* emphasized the centrality of *jihad* as a unifying mechanism for the community, the importance of which transcended the petty leadership squabbles of the early community. They were fairly quickly marginalized in mainstream Islamic history.

Characteristically, most of this analysis has demonstrated a tendency to interpret the meaning of 9/11 in cosmic terms—a Manichean struggle between good and evil in which the forces, though fairly evenly matched, are stacked slightly in favor of the evil. Less consideration has been given to conceptualizing the al-Qa'ida organization in more concrete, less metaphysical terms—that is, as a smallish (although perhaps large as far as these organizations generally go) paranoiac, extremist, right-wing (in Islamic terms) militia group led primarily by alienated veterans of the Afghan war against the Soviet occupation of the 1980s, augmented by other naïve enthusiasts for whom the "romantic" notion of *jihad* has at least temporarily captured their imaginations. Paranoiac, extremist, right- or left-wing organizations seldom represent the "default" mindset of any country or society. Such groups become truly dangerous when they gain actual state power as did the Bolsheviks in Russia in 1917 or the Nazis in Germany in 1933. Al-Qa'ida had not reached that position by 11 September 2001—even in Afghanistan—and is less likely to do so now. To say this is not to say that such groups cannot commit dangerous acts. They obviously can and do. In this commentator's view, however, it is useful to avoid according such groups any great significance, or to attribute to them importance they do not deserve.

---

[1] Dean of the School of Intelligence Studies, Joint Military Intelligence College, and Middle East scholar and intelligence analyst.

In this study, the author has focused on a particular aspect of Islam—namely the concept of *jihad* — as the troublesome feature of the religion that, if permitted to flourish, poses a long-term threat to America. To rephrase his argument, Islam, a religion aimed at facilitating the emergence of a peaceful political order among its believers, cannot really achieve its destiny unless most or all of humanity accepts its tenets or submits to the authority of its political leadership(s). The message of Islam, according to the author, informs its adherents that the world outside of itself is inherently hostile, and Muslims must always be prepared to be at war with it. Conflict between the Islamic and non-Islamic worlds is therefore, in the author's view, inevitable and can be marked at best by only temporary truces. America currently is the leading power of the non-Islamic world and therefore an "existential" enemy of Islam, at least as conceived by the al-Qa'ida militants, a situation highlighted by the attacks of September 11. The attacks were made by a rising generation of young militant Muslims inspired by the Islamic doctrine of *jihad* (struggle, or exertion, in the path of Allah) who, funded by oil wealth and charitable contributions from throughout the Islamic world, and disillusioned with existing leaderships in that same universe, seek to lead a movement that can capture the imagination of the Muslim masses, revive the ultimately global mission of the Islamic enterprise, and achieve global domination. America, as the leading global power, is the principal obstacle to achieving this end, and its superpower status must eventually be countered, neutralized, and eventually overcome for the jihadists to achieve their aim. The jihadists, therefore, also pose an existential threat to America, or at least its superpower status.

The author does not argue that all or even most Muslims currently understand or advocate this radical worldview, but he does hold that it represents the true teaching of Islam, which has not yet experienced a "reformation." In this regard, he concurs with the perspective of the jihadists about Islam, although he does point out the limitations of this point of view. He also argues that support for this view and more particularly the exploits of the jihadists is probably more widespread throughout the Islamic world than we care to imagine, and continued successful operations by the jihadists will only garner more support. The problem, therefore, is potentially larger than just the concept of *jihad*, but lies with Islam itself, for which *jihad* is an integral concept.

Nor does the author hold that the goal of the jihadists is inevitable, although the argument is typically Manichean in its implications—either we will prevail, or the Muslim world will prevail. He does argue that the movement is an autonomous one. Negotiated settlements of specific conflicts, such as those in Algeria, Kashmir, Chechnya, the Balkans, Central Asia, Southeast Asia, and/or Israel/Palestine will have no impact on the struggle. The goal is world domination, no more and no less. Indeed, the local *jihads* in each of these areas must be successfully defeated and eliminated. Only by total and compelling defeat can the threat posed by Islamic *jihad* be neutralized. In general the author in his analysis does not recognize any other underlying aspect to these conflicts than the cause of Islam.

The author is sensitive to the fact that *jihad* is a complex term that can be understood in a number of different ways. Traditional Islamic jurisprudence distinguishes between two major levels of *jihad*. The Greater *Jihad* refers to the inner struggle of the individual believer to affirm his or her commitment to the requirements of Islam, and is also called *jihad* of the heart. It is the Lesser *Jihad*, or *jihad* of the sword (often translated "holy war," a translation the author scrupulously avoids) that is the central concern of his study. Sometimes called the "sixth pillar of Islam," there is no question that *jihad* is a required commitment of the Muslim. Moreover, although most Qur'anic verses define it as the collective responsibility all Muslims to defend the community against non-Muslim aggressors, there are a few verses, as well as *hadith* (authentic traditions ascribed to the Prophet Muhammad), that can be interpreted to justify wars of imperial conquest. It is also certainly true that at various times in Islamic history conquerors have used the concept of *jihad* to justify imperial expansion. For most of Islamic history, however, as the author also notes, the concept of *jihad* as an animator of war against non-Muslims has lain dormant, or more correctly according to Islamic jurisprudence, temporarily suspended for tactical reasons through the medium of formal truces of definite or indefinite duration because of the weakness of Islamic power. Ensuring that Muslim jurists perceive the necessity of keeping the call for *jihad* in suspension should become therefore a principal goal of U.S. planners, according to the author.

Those who are familiar with the writings and speeches of Sayyed Qutb, Abdullah al-Azzam, Osama Bin Laden, and other notable proponents of the militant Islamic perspective (sources the author has not extensively used) are acquainted with the arguments about Islam made in this study. The author is indeed representing their views correctly, but is the perspective of the militants as pervasive as the author suggests? I would suggest that it is not. U.S. soldiers serving in Afghanistan in relatively small numbers were quite aware that they were surrounded by and lending support to Muslim allies engaged in conflict with other Muslim opponents (that is, the Taliban and al-Qa'ida). Similarly in Iraq, although the circumstances are very different, the U.S. is technically supporting Muslim allies against other Muslim opponents. If we engage in other Muslim countries in the future, the same circumstance will also be true. So the conflict in which the United States finds itself engaged in the Islamic world is not as clear-cut as the author suggests. Indeed, by our recent interventions in Afghanistan and Iraq, and with possibly more to come, we may even be unintentionally evoking and encouraging the very jihadist response the author seeks to warn us about. Much depends on the policies we pursue in the Islamic world as well as how our "counter-jihad" analysts understand the religion and culture of the realm in which we are operating.

In the class on Islam I have been teaching at the Joint Military Intelligence College for the past 20 years, and before that at George Washington University, I make use of a visual graphic entitled "Correct Values." It purports to represent the key values I believe Islamic teaching, doctrine and law attempt to inculcate in the believer. It does not necessarily reflect those values that members of Muslim society may actually display—hypocrisy is not the sole property of other religious traditions—rather, it attempts to highlight those values Muslims generally would agree characterize the "good Muslim."

The nine values represent the limitations of modern visual technology rather than any effort to conclude that the good Muslim should exhibit just these nine characteristics. Perhaps the number is 90; perhaps it is more; perhaps it is fewer. In attempting to tease out nine idealistic characteristics that would fit on a power point slide, the present author settled on these nine after considerable reflection and study.

Correct Values

Piety	(Continuous Consciousness of God
Humility	(Consciousness of Dependence on God)
Honesty	(With God, Others, Oneself)
Respectfulness	(All men are equal before God)
Cooperation	(Competition is a Source of Conflict)
Courage	(To Strive in the Path of Islam)
Mercifulness	(Correct Use of Power and Authority)
Generosity	(Reflection of God's Generosity)
Justice	(The Foundation of Social Unity)

A key point to be made here is that the concept of *jihad* is not among these values (unless one focuses on the value of courage). Nor are there on the list such values as martyrdom, cowardice, vengeance, retaliation, cruelty, murder, terrorism, or other related characteristics that are sometimes associated stereotypically with Islam by various non-Muslim commentators seeking to define the nature of the Islamic threat against those who are not part of the Islamic world. Seen from an Islamic point of view, the role of jihad (struggle in the way of Allah), like the other five pillars of Islam, is to aid the believer in realizing these values. If the achievement of justice, therefore, is a value to be upheld, then the requirement to struggle against perceived injustice or oppression can result in conflict that from a Muslim perspective is wholly justified. What constitutes justice and injustice is, of course, a matter of interpretation and may be subject to negotiation.

U.S. forces operating in the Islamic world can benefit from at least being aware of these values. In general, they are universal values that are not difficult to uphold, at least on an ethical basis. Efforts to demonstrate that U.S. policy upholds these values can go a long way toward cultivating cooperative relations or at least neutralizing opposition. On the other hand, demonstrations of impiety, arrogance, dishonesty, disrespect, a patronizing attitude, cowardice, mercilessness, misanthropy, or injustice are almost guaranteed to evoke the opposition of religiously minded Muslims who by the obligation of jihad are likely to resist American initiatives.

Such is likely to be at least part of the advice of the well-qualified counter-jihad analyst advocated by the author in this essay. I indeed agree with him that a cadre of analysts well-trained and knowledgeable concerning the intricacies of Islamic law and doctrine needs to be a part of the emerging intelligence force of the 21st century. I disagree with his charge that such a cadre cannot be found in the U.S. universities. This does not mean that enhanced education and training about Islam should not also occur in the Intelligence Community. An "Islam in the Contemporary World" course has been offered at the Joint Military Intelligence College for the past 20 years. Many military intelligence officers and civilian analysts who had other majors in College or otherwise had no exposure to this topic, have completed this course over the years. Hopefully, the Intelligence Community as a whole benefits from the continuing existence of this course, although that benefit is hard to define or measure. Undoubtedly much more could be done. A single course such as this cannot produce Islamic "specialists."

This said, the author is quite correct in identifying a body of Muslims who uphold the militant jihadist ideology he explicates, especially in his treatment of "The Operational Threat." They are declared enemies of the United States and have displayed their enmity openly and on a number of occasions. Whether they number only a few thousand at most, as I would assert, or several million, as the author suggests, there remain upward of 1.2 billion other Muslims worldwide, most of whom are not politically motivated, do not share the same view of *jihad*, and seek mainly to live their lives in peace and security— within an Islamic context, to be sure. The jihadists are also enemies of this vast majority of Muslims whom they routinely condemn as *kafirs* (infidels), if they fail to accept the jihadist point of view. In my opinion, the vast majority of Muslims will welcome their demise and would not welcome the demise of the United States. Nevertheless, a good understanding of Islam and Islamic "culture" is required for the United States to wend its way through the shoals of potential misunderstanding in dealing with the Islamic world.

Accordingly, I agree with the author's view that the counterterrorist paradigm is insufficient to cope with the threat posed by this jihadist-animated cadre. These individuals are engaged on a global basis in a hearts-and-mind struggle to win the support and adulation of the larger Islamic world, and far more than sporadic acts of terrorism against U.S. or other non-Muslim, or even Muslim, targets is required for them to achieve this goal. A cadre of intelligence specialists with special expertise in Islamic affairs could make a positive contribution in assisting U.S. policymakers as they deal with a challenge posed by jihadists that transcends the concerns of the typical counterterrorism analyst.

Is America at risk because of the threat posed by the Islamic jihadists? Well, September 11 demonstrated that we are. But I also think we err if we exaggerate the threat. Unlike the author, I think the real strategic center of gravity of the jihadists may lie among those of us who convince ourselves that they represent the true face of Islam. We must work with our millions of other Muslim allies in the Islamic world to demonstrate and to convince ourselves that they do not.

GLOBAL WAR ON TERRORISM: THE STRATEGIC THREAT

AMERICA'S CHALLENGE

Islam generally divides the world into two "houses," the "house of Islam" and the "house of war." Although not of its own choice, the U.S. as the sole remaining super-power, and a non-Muslim state, is the modern leader of the "house of war." The context of Islam's duality and the unavoidable threat it poses to U.S. national security can be understood through the lens of lifelong scholars. The Intelligence Community must orient itself to this menace.

Generally, Islam is peaceful within the "house of Islam"; however, it is prepared to extend itself into the "house of war" by force or *"Jihad"* (extensively discussed later). "This bipartite division of the world into an abode of peace and an abode of war finds a parallel in the communistic theory of Soviet Russia."[1] Historically, there have been periods when Islam has abandoned forceful expansion, or has made accommodations that, at least temporarily, provide a middle ground between the two "houses." Generally, when Islam is on the advance, Jihad accelerates, and when the spread of Islam is on the decline, it stops. Given the undesirability of a conflict between the U.S. and Islam, it is imperative that U.S. policymakers understand the threat that comes with leading the "house of war," while maintaining awareness of the historical middle-ground.

Not all Muslims are jihadists, but, all jihadists are Muslims. Jihadists must be understood for whom they are, and why they enjoy broad support within the Muslim world. They are not criminals or terrorists; they are strugglers and soldiers in the path of Allah. Who is a criminal or murderer/terrorist is a moral judgment. Usama bin Laden (UBL) is a genuine Muslim hero. Thou shall not steal and thou shall not murder are commandments shared by Jews, Christians, and Muslims. Therefore, whether one has broken one of those commandments is theologically based. Jihadists view themselves, by definition, as being on the highest moral plane as they struggle in the path of Allah. Their actions, within the rules of Jihad (discussed later) therefore are moral, required, and legal. Furthermore, as the beholders of the true religion, they have the right to expand; opposition is immoral, wicked, and evil. Muslims everywhere, should the social and military situation allow, must assert their independence or autonomy from rule not based on Islamic law. Thus, Muslims create their own victimization, which must be avenged. In fact, opposition to Islamic violence or Jihad, as seen by Muslims, amounts to repression, which must be answered by increased violence, or "defensive Jihad" (discussed later). The West, failing to come to terms with this new threat, and treating jihadist behavior as either criminal or "terrorist," is ill-prepared to deal with it.

---

[1] Philip K. Hitti, *History of the Arabs: From the Earliest Times to the Present,* 9th ed. (New York: St Martin's Press, 1968), 138

Arab governments in particular, and Muslim governments in general, have for generations laid the foundation of hatred, anti-Semitism, and victimization that has led to support for jihadists, even against their own government. Those very governments, after becoming "enemies" of Islam, lost credibility when they failed to act. This gave opportunity for others, in the name of Islam, to fight when legitimate Muslim rulers refused to do so, or when they dared to collaborate with the U.S. or Israel. They thus wrested the mantle of the "legitimate callers for Jihad" from Muslim rulers. Muslim rulers' attempts to placate Islamists by giving them control of educational and social welfare programs were fatally flawed. Their efforts to separate what in Islam is inseparable — religion and governance — resulted in religious extremists being in charge of youth education and human welfare. Just as "Hitler Youth," indoctrinated in Nazi ideology since birth, defended the Fuehrer's bunker to the end, so will a large segment of Muslims similarly indoctrinated in Jihad and anti-Western and anti-Semitic beliefs support the modern Jihad. Just as most "normal" Germans supported the Nazis when they appeared to be victorious, until the destruction that Hitler brought to Germany became obvious, the general Muslim populations will support Jihad until they are convinced that it is militarily futile, at least at this time, to attack the West.

The jihadist threat is not a national, but a global Muslim one. It is one of religion (in the Islamic sense), not of politics (in the Western sense). It is not founded on any specific act that the U.S. does or does not undertake. Therefore, leaving Muslim lands or "solving" the Israeli-Palestinian conflict, will not end the problem. Jihad exists where there are Muslims, and conditions allow. To stoke the fires of Jihad, after Israel-Palestine and U.S. withdrawal from the "Muslim lands," there is still Chechnya, Kashmir, the Balkans, Central Asia, Afghanistan, and Indonesia/Malaysia/Philippines. In addition, all Arab countries, and some other Muslim countries, have one degree or another of jihadist movement. This is today's list; tomorrow's list will have additions.

The late Philip K. Hitti, renowned Princeton (and earlier Columbia University) Orientalist, wrote the following last paragraph in his comprehensive work on the history of the Arabs:

> Originators of the third monotheistic religion, beneficiaries of the other two, co-sharers with the West of the Greco-Roman cultural tradition, holders aloft of the torch of enlightenment throughout medieval times, generous contributors to European renaissance, the Arabic-speaking peoples have taken their place among the awakened, forward-marching independent nations of the modern world. With their rich heritage and unmatched natural resource of oil, they should be able to make a significant contribution to the material and spiritual progress of mankind.[2]

---

[2] Hitti, *History of the Arabs: From the Earliest Times to the Present*, 757.

Immediately before this paragraph, he expressed the view that "Of all the Arab republics of the area, Lebanon has been the most stable."[3] This summation was penned by a scholar of the region, and a Christian Lebanese, less than ten years before what would ultimately become a religiously based civil war that destroyed Lebanon. Political predictions in the Middle East are often short-lived. What is constant is Islam.

Hitti's wish has yet to come true. It is not impossible to achieve, but must be prefaced by a fundamental change, or reformation in Islam. Tolerance for other religions, not just those subjugated to Islam, but those under their own authority, must be accepted. Jihad, as a military option, must be abandoned as an aspect of the religion. All those within Islam who seek equality and participation must be allowed to do so. Until then, the U.S. must be reconciled that the modern Jihad must be understood to be fought successfully. A reformation of Islam will only come about when the *Umma* — all Muslims regardless of race or class, to which must be added gender — see the futility of violence, and the benefits of Hitti's "dream."

---

[3] Hitti, *History of the Arabs: From the Earliest Times to the Present,* 757.

THE GLOBAL WAR ON TERRORISM, THAT ISN'T

11 September 2001 (9/11) is a defining day in U.S. history. The shock of the attack on the World Trade Center (WTC) in New York, and on the Pentagon in Washington DC, is often compared to the Japanese attack on Pearl Harbor on 7 December 1941. Both, from a U.S. perspective, are seen as "sneak attacks." From a strategic perspective, however, neither should be so considered. In 1941 it was obvious that the U.S. and Japan were on a collision course. In fact, negotiations to "defuse" the situation were ongoing when Pearl Harbor was attacked. The "sneak attack" on Pearl Harbor occurred on the operational level. An attack on the Philippines was considered more likely. The attack on the WTC and the Pentagon came as a strategic surprise. Despite prior attacks from Al-Qa'ida, the U.S. did not consider itself at war. The failure of 9/11 should have been an operational/tactical one; instead it was strategic. "Connecting the dots" is therefore not the proper concept to use to highlight an alleged "intelligence failure." What the intelligence/law enforcement community failed to do to prevent 9/11 was closer to putting together the pieces of a jigsaw puzzle. What made assembling the pieces that much harder is that a "picture" of the finished puzzle was not available. What was missing was the strategic context; that is, the big-picture threat that the U.S. faced. Fundamental to this omission was and is the Intelligence Community's (IC's) predilection to deal with counterterrorism on the operational/tactical level. Al-Qa'ida, however, is not a terrorist organization. It is an Islamic Jihadist organization that has declared Jihad against the U.S. U.S. references to a "Global War on Terrorism (GWOT)," mischaracterize the threat; we face an Islamic Jihad. This does not mean (as it may have 1,400 years ago) that the U.S. is at war with Islam. It does, however, mean that a portion of Islam considers itself in a Jihad against the U.S. Part of the professional responsibility of strategic intelligence analysis is to provide the context or "big picture" of this war, and thereby to paint the "picture" which will help clarify the operational/tactical intelligence analysis.

Complicating a Western capability to understand the war that has been thrust upon it is a profound lack of historical awareness in modern society. The West lives in the twenty-first century, looking eagerly toward the twenty-second. Many in the Muslim world live in the seventeenth century looking longingly toward the seventh century. If we compare Western and Islamic political language, we shall find that they have much in common.

> But despite these resemblances, there are still enormous differences, and these are particularly clear in the language of political assertion, denunciation, and appeal. Muslims revere different scriptures — not the Bible but the Qur'an. They are nurtured on different classics, and draw inspiration and guidance from a different history. Few if any civilizations in the past have attached as much importance to history as did Islam, in its education, in its awareness of itself, in the common language of everyday talk. Even...in the

war...between Iraq and Iran [1980-88], the war propaganda of both sides makes frequent allusions to events of the seventh and eighth centuries.[4]

In the modern Western world the concept of religious warfare is relegated to the Reformation, or more likely a dim memory of the Crusades. In Islam, Jihad is a living part of the faith. The West, therefore views religion in only one aspect: the peaceful relationship of a community of faithful to their maker, or more broadly an individual's belief system. Islam, however, has a political component absent in other religions. "In contrast to Western sympathizers and Western-influenced modernists who argue that Islam has nothing to do with politics, Khomeini observes that 'the Qur'an contains a hundred times more verses concerning social problems than on devotional subjects. Out of fifty books of Muslim tradition there are perhaps three or four which deal with prayer or with man's duties toward God, a few on morality and all the rest have to do with society, economics, law, politics and the state....' Islam, according to the same authority, 'is political or it is nothing.' A significant and growing number of Muslims in many countries agree with him."[5]

Bitter experience has taught the Christian world that should a government attempt to regulate religion, it opens itself to repressive regimes, or brutal warfare.

> The history of Christianity is much concerned with schism and heresy, and with conflicts in which the proponents of competing doctrines and the wielders of rival authorities struggled to overcome each other, by persecution when this was feasible, by war when it was not.... [G]rowing numbers of Christians finally concluded that only by depriving the churches of access to the coercive and repressive powers of the state, and by depriving the state of the power to intervene in the affairs of the church, could they achieve any tolerable coexistence between people of differing faiths and creeds. The Muslim experience was very different. Muslims had of course their religious disagreements, and these on occasion led to strife and repression. But there is nothing remotely comparable with such epoch-making Christian events as the Schism of Photius, the Reformation, the Holy Office of the Inquisition, and the bloody religious wars of the sixteenth and seventeenth centuries, which almost compelled Christians to secularize their states and societies in order to escape from the vicious cycle of persecution and conflict. Muslims encountered no such problems, and therefore required no such solution.[6]

Religious freedom and toleration has therefore become central to "Western values."

It is in this context that Islam is viewed as a "peaceful religion." Islam has not, however, undergone a reformation, and still retains the duality of its origins: a peaceful dar al-Islam

---

[4] Bernard Lewis, *The Political Language of Islam* (Chicago: The University of Chicago Press, 1988), 9.

[5] Bernard Lewis, *Islam in History,* 2nd ed. (Chicago: Open Court Publishing Company, 2001), 403.

[6] Bernard Lewis, *What Went Wrong* (New York: Oxford University Press, 2002), 103-104.

(Muslim territory or house) confronting the dar al-Harb (territory or house of the enemy). "The world was divided into the House of Islam, where the Muslim faith and law prevailed, and the House of War, where they did not, and between the two there would be a perpetual state of war, interrupted only by truces, until the Word of God was brought to all humanity. For most Muslim writers, Christendom — first Byzantine and then European — was the House of War par excellence."[7]

> Militance and peaceableness exist side by side in Islam, and Muhammad practiced both of them. After settling in Medina, he took up the struggle against Mecca and later extended it to other adversaries. Pagans were forced to accept Islam and agreements were made with the People of the Book, i.e., primarily Jews and Christians, provided they were willing to live under Muslim rule. They enjoyed a certain degree of religious freedom, but were obliged to pay special taxes. The basis for this can be found in sura [Qur'anic verse] 9:29, which states that war against those who have received Scriptures must be waged "until they pay the tribute out of hand and have been humbled."[8]

This is the why a Jewish State of Israel, as well as a Christian State of Lebanon, are and were unacceptable, and why a dominant United States is intolerable. Western analysts and policymakers, unaccustomed to dealing with this duality, thereby fail to understand today's strategic threat.

---

[7] Bernard Lewis, *Cultures in Conflict* (New York: Oxford University Press, 1995), 14.

[8] Heribert Busse, *Islam, Judaism, and Christianity*, trans. Allison Brown (Princeton, NJ: Markus Weiner Publishers, 1998), 141.

THE STRATEGIC THREAT

During the Cold War the Intelligence Community analyzed the strategic threat from the Soviet Union. The question was always asked as to how the Soviets would react to a certain situation or how a given event might fit into the overall strategic picture. The world was viewed through the prism of how any action or event would impact the overall U.S./Soviet military balance or political relationship. It could be, and has been argued that viewing the world in this manner led the U.S. to take "incorrect" actions by overestimating, or underestimating, Soviet equities in certain circumstances. The war against communism and then against a Soviet Union that combined a communist economic system with a totalitarian political one, was an existential[9] one for the U.S. When Nikita Krushchev said that he would bury the U.S. he was referring to forcing a fundamental change in our economic and political system. Fortunately for the world, the Soviets were so convinced of the inevitability of their victory because of the superiority of communism over capitalism that burying the U.S. could be accomplished as a gradual process. The large nuclear arsenals of the antagonists also made a direct military confrontation unpalatable. The Cold War was fought on the periphery, by seeking political, military and economic advantage. Because the U.S. realized that the Cold War was an existential one, all other considerations were secondary. Regimes that the U.S. would not ordinarily want to support, and wars that the U.S. was not eager to fight within the context of the Cold War, became necessary. It was this basic assessment of the strategic threat that drove U.S. policy. Thus, the 1979 Soviet invasion of Afghanistan was not viewed in the context of a war between two neighboring states, but as a continuation of a Russian Czarist push toward warm-water ports in the Persian Gulf and Arabian Sea. Halting the Soviet advance was not viewed in the context of protecting Afghanistan, but in terms of how a Soviet victory there would impact the Cold War. The U.S. is again in an existential battle, however gradual, and must understand the strategic threat in order to take appropriate actions.

To understand the nature of the threat only one question needs to be answered: What would the U.S. surrender document look like? Can it be cloaked in "Vietnamization" in which one can gradually disengage, watch an ally lose, and suffer no threat to the U.S. homeland? Or, will the jihadists demand something more far-reaching? On the surface, Al-Qa'ida may appear to fit into the mold of "traditional" terrorist groups of the 1970s and 1980s: agree to their political demands, and peace can be bought. "One man's terrorist is another man's freedom fighter" has often proved a correct characterization. Al-Qa'ida jihadists, however, are not freedom fighters; they are warriors "in the path of God." Their "political demands" are rooted in two declarations, one made by the Al-Qa'ida leader Usama bin Laden in 1996, and another issued in a fatwa [a Muslim religious opinion] in 1998.

At the heart of bin Laden's philosophy are two declarations of war or Jihad against the United States. The first, his Bayan (statement) issued on 26 August 1996, was directed

---

[9] "Existential" is used here in the following sense: threatening the existence of the U.S. as a capitalist and democratic country governed by its Constitution.

specifically at "Americans occupying the land of the two holy places," as bin Laden refers to the cities of Mecca and Medina that are located in his native Saudi Arabia. Here he calls upon Muslims all over the world to fight to "expel the infidels...from the Arab Peninsula." In his fatwa of 23 February 1998, titled "Declaration of the World Islamic Front for Jihad Against the Jews and Crusaders," which he issued along with the leaders of extremist groups in Egypt, Pakistan, and Bangladesh, bin Laden broadened his earlier edict. In the fatwa, he specifies that the radicals' war is a defensive struggle against Americans and their allies who have declared war "on God, his messenger, and Muslims." The "crimes and sins" perpetrated by the United States are threefold: first, it "stormed" the Arabian peninsula during the Gulf War and has continued "occupying the lands of Islam in their holiest of places"; second, it continues a war of annihilation against Iraq; and third, the United States supports the state of Israel and its continued occupation of Jerusalem.[10]

On their face the political demands of this "terrorist" group seem straightforward. To surrender and achieve peace the U.S. must: remove all forces from the Arabian Peninsula (this means not only Saudi Arabia, but all of the Gulf States and Yemen); leave Iraq; and stop supporting Israel. However improbable this may be, it appears *prima facie* that this is not an existential decision for the U.S. It may, however, represent an existential decision for Israel and Arab governments that support the U.S. Agreeing to this "surrender document" will not, however, bring the U.S. peace with the jihadists. It, at best, will bring a "truce" [hudna]. "'*I have been ordered to fight the people until they say: None has the right to be worshiped but Allah.*' Therefore, when non-Muslims embrace Islam, all war activities against them must cease and come to an end."[11]

A real peace treaty between the U.S. and the Jihadists is simple, and is based on the Islamic religious law (shari'a) of Jihad. "Failure by non-Muslims to accept Islam or pay the poll tax made it incumbent on the Muslim state to declare a Jihad upon the recalcitrant individuals and communities."[12] "The polytheists have the limited choice between Islam or the Jihad; the scriptuaries [peoples of the book] can chose one of three propositions: Islam, the poll tax [jizya], or the Jihad. If they accept Islam, they are entitled under the law to full citizenship as other believers; if they prefer to remain scriptuaries at the sacrifice of paying the poll tax, they suffer certain disabilities which reduce them to second-class citizens; if they fight they are to be treated in war on the same footing as polytheists."[13] For the jihadists, the U.S. must either accept Islam, accept a poll tax or die in a Jihad. The poll tax, however, if paid as a tribute will invoke the shari'a for peace treaties, and not end the Jihad, but only a postponment of it. To end the Jihad the U.S. must either accept Islam, or pay a poll tax as "peoples of the book" (dhimmis) under the "protection"

---

[10] Michael G. Knapp, *"The Concept and Practice of Jihad in Islam," Parameters 33*, no. 1 (Spring 2003), 90.

[11] Jalal Abualrub, *Holy War Crusades Jihad: In the Torah, the Gospels, and the Quran*, ed. Alaa Mencke (Orlando: Madinah Publishers and Distributors, 2002), 281.

[12] Majid Khadduri, *War and Peace in the Law of Islam* (Baltimore: The Johns Hopkins Press, 1955), 53.

[13] Khadduri, *War and Peace in the Law of Islam*, 80.

of Islam. Either option is an unacceptable existential choice. This is the strategic threat that the Intelligence Community must make clear to U.S. policymakers. Identifying centers of gravity and understanding the nature of the enemy flows from understanding the strategic threat. Analysis of the operational and tactical threats also flows from a thorough understanding of the strategic threat.

Islam is a universalist religion. As Muhammad was the "seal of the prophets," Islam is viewed by its adherents as the final true religion. It is only through Islam that paradise can be achieved, and its predecessor religions, Judaism and Christianity, although valid for their time, are superceded by Islam. "Traditional Christianity and Islam differed from Judaism and agreed with each other in that both claimed to possess not only universal but exclusive truths. Each claimed to be the sole custodian of God's final revelation to mankind. Neither admitted salvation outside of its own creed."[14] "The Jewish perception of the religious other is different from that shared by Christians and Muslims...while Jews claim that the truths of their faith are universal, they do not claim that they are exclusive. Judaism is for Jews and those who care to join them. But, according to a well-known Talmudic dictum, the righteous of all peoples and faith have their place in paradise."[15] "When Christians and Muslims called each other accursed infidels, each understood exactly what the other meant, because each meant exactly the same thing.... More recently, many — though by no means all — Christian churches and theologians have relinquished this claim to exclusive truth and have begun to use the term "triumphalism" to denote and denounce it. There has yet been no corresponding change among the authorized spokesmen of Islam."[16] In fact, modern jihadists have reemphasized the Islamization of all mankind, and invigorated a militant concept of Jihad to ensure their success.

Ironically, the modern Western world against which the jihadists rail has been the enabler of their global Jihad. Instant communication and airplane transportation have allowed the establishment of a global Jihad network. The ability of all Muslims to simultaneously unite in a single cause has not existed since the early Caliphs when Islam was geographically confined to the Arabian Peninsula. Today funds and personnel can traverse the earth in operationally significant timeframes. Jihadists, such as Al-Qa'ida, view it as their religious obligation to take advantage of what Allah has provided. Although many Jihads have been fought since the advent of Islam, they were never fought on as many fronts as is seen today. Fortunately, today's Jihads are not universally recognized, nor supported. It is the jihadists' aim to eventually use the tools currently available to unite all Muslims in a Jihad to bring Islam to all humankind.

The timeframe of the Jihad, and its level of ferocity, greatly differs from that which the U.S. faced during the Cold War. The Soviets/Communists and the jihadists both believe that, in the former, history was on their side; in the latter, that Allah will ensure their victory. The Soviets were not pressed for time and built their military-industrial complex as they chal-

---

[14] Bernard Lewis, Islam and the West (New York: Oxford University Press, 1993), 175.
[15] Lewis, Islam and the West, 175.
[16] Lewis, Islam and the West, 175-176.

lenged the U.S. globally. All-out confrontation was both unnecessary and undesirable. The jihadist, on the other hand, has a personal stake in the course of the Jihad. Waiting for future generations to achieve victory is not the preferred option. To the jihadist, their personal place in Paradise is directly linked to their performance in the Jihad. The U.S. is thus faced with an enemy that wants to inflict maximum damage, as soon as possible.

As bleak as the prospect of having to fight in a Jihad may appear, there is the possibility of limiting the effectiveness of the jihadists, while fashioning a "reformation" of Islam. This "reformation," must be revolutionary, but also based upon accommodation rather than conflict with the West. The U.S. is not fighting the entire Muslim world. On the other hand, jihadists in general, and Al-Qa'ida in particular, have strong support among Muslims. They could not have been as successful as they have been without it. This support has ranged from political cover, to moral support, to the provision of safe haven and financial aid. Al-Qa'ida operatives, unlike traditional terrorist groups, can find such support globally. Driven by Arab money and Wahhabi theology, Jihad is growing in Africa (east and west), Central Asia, the Far East, and Europe. In fact, its prospects for immediate success are greater in those areas than in an Arab world where regimes have confronted the threat. The objectives of Al-Qa'ida are, and must be, universally (with only fringe but notable exceptions) accepted by Islam. Their methods, and the legality of their call for Jihad, are not, however, near to being universally accepted. It is in these two areas, the legality of this particular Jihad, and their methods, including the killing of "innocent" civilians and other Muslims, along with their use of suicide operatives, that Al-Qa'ida, and all jihadists, can be challenged. U.S. policymakers must be aware of the strength of the universal appeal of the jihadist message amongst Muslims, and also of the "flaws" of the jihadist methods under Shari'a. These are the strategic centers of gravity of Al-Qa'ida and the jihadists. Other centers of gravity that have heretofore been considered strategic, such as the provision of safe haven and finances, are in fact operational considerations.

The U.S. must also be able to identify the "enemy." Al-Qa'ida is not a "terrorist" organization; in fact it is not a close-knit organization at all. It is the rallying point for one of the two current concepts of modern Jihad. Until Al-Qa'ida's declaration of war against the U.S. and Jews, depending on the group, jihadist movements had initial limited objectives of overthrowing the government in a specific Muslim country and establishing an Islamic country ruled by shari'a. Al-Qa'ida takes a broader view of the issue, in that it supports a global Jihad. This Jihad includes those local ones, but also is a continuation of the Jihad that destroyed the Soviet Union, and will destroy America, and thus open the way for the establishment of Islam as the world religion. Al-Qa'ida thus represents an idea that is fundamental to Islam, and was historically played out in the conquest of the Persian and Byzantine Empires. U.S. efforts to combat the global Jihad being waged against it is based on the idea that far from all Muslims believe that now is the time for Jihad. Thus, the U.S. faces a situation similar to that which existed during the Vietnam War, when there were Vietnamese on its side, Vietnamese who supported North Vietnam and the Viet Cong, and Vietnamese who appeared to be in one category, but in fact were in the other. Although few Muslims are active supporters of Al-Qa'ida, all members of Al-Qa'ida and their supporters are Muslim. To win this war the U.S. will be forced to rely on Muslim governmental and individual support. Key to victory lies in determining how best to win that support, and to understand the limitations of that support.

Muslim, and more particularly, Arab pride is central to how the U.S. is viewed. Arabs, for centuries have been angered by their impotence and weakness. Thus, Islam aside, there will be hatred in the Arab world of the U.S. based upon U.S. strength. Therefore, without a cultural "sea change" the U.S. cannot win the "hearts and minds" of a large segment of traditional Arab culture. Jihadists will play upon this hatred, mixed with their jihadist theories, to inflame popular opinion against the U.S.

> For a long time now there has been a rising tide of rebellion against this Western paramountcy, and a desire to reassert Muslim values and restore Muslim greatness. The Muslim has suffered successive stages of defeat. The first was his loss of domination in the world, to the advancing power of Russia and the West. The second was the undermining of his authority in his own country, through an invasion of foreign ideas and laws and ways of life and sometimes even foreign rulers or settlers, and the enfranchisement of native non-Muslim elements. The third — the last straw — was the challenge to his mastery in his own house, from emancipated women and rebellious children. It was too much to endure, and the outbreak of rage against these alien, infidel, and incomprehensible forces that had subverted his dominance, disrupted his society, and finally violated the sanctity of his home was inevitable.[17]

As U.S. forces become more involved in directly conducting security operations in Muslim lands, the very nature of these operations will alienate Muslims. Muslim men, however impotent externally, view themselves as omnipotent in their households. Routine searches, especially in front of their families, will be viewed as an insult to their manhood. The ultimate insult would be the searching of their women and children, a fact that those who wish to do the U.S. harm will take advantage of. Normal force protection measures will therefore just tend to create hatred for the U.S. If this hatred is not accompanied by a commensurate fear, U.S. forces will be continuously attacked.

> But why the hostility in the first place? If we turn from the general to the specific, there is no lack of individual policies and actions, pursued and taken by individual Western governments, that have aroused the passionate anger of Middle Eastern and other Islamic peoples. Yet, when these policies are abandoned and the problems resolved, there is only a local and temporary alleviation. The French have left Algeria, the British have left Egypt, the Western oil companies have left their oil wells, the westernizing Shah has left Iran — yet the generalized resentment of the fundamentalists and other extremists against the West and its friends remains and grows and is not appeased.... What is truly evil and unacceptable is the domination of infidels over true

---

[17] Bernard Lewis, "The Roots of Muslim Rage," *The Atlantic* 266, no 3, (September 1990), URL: <*http://www.theatlantic.com/issues/90sep/rage.htm*>, accessed 19 December 2002.

believers. For true believers to rule misbelievers is proper and natural, since this provides for the maintenance of the holy law, and gives the misbelievers both the opportunity and the incentive to embrace the true faith. But for misbelievers to rule over true believers is blasphemous and unnatural, since it leads to the corruption of religion and morality in society, and to the flouting or even the abrogation of God's law... It may also explain why spokesmen for the new Muslim minorities in Western Europe demand for Islam a degree of legal protection which those countries no longer give to Christianity and have never given to Judaism....The true faith, based on God's final revelation, must be protected from insult and abuse; other faiths, being either false or incomplete, have no right to any such protection.... In our own time this mood of admiration [for the West] and emulation has, among many Muslims, given way to one of hostility and rejection. In part this mood is surely due to a feeling of humiliation — a growing awareness, among the heirs of an old, proud, and long-dominant civilization, of having been overtaken, overborne, and overwhelmed by those whom they regarded as inferiors.[18]

Even more humiliating than having been overtaken by the West is the realization that the West, and the U.S. in particular, is needed to protect Muslims. Thus, little or no credit is given to the U.S. for liberating Kuwait, for by doing so the U.S. defeated a Muslim country, Iraq, and furthermore two Muslim countries, Kuwait, and more importantly Saudi Arabia, had to rely on the U.S. for their security. This is an explanation as to why the U.S. is not "thanked" for its intervention, on behalf of Muslims, in the Balkans.

Many among those who believe in the Biblical texts under discussion [those that condone the killing of non-combatants] efficiently implemented them throughout their history....The contemporary disaster that struck Muslims of *Bosnia* is another example. For more than three years, from April 1992 to December 1995, the Christian World stood by silently, watching their fellow Christian *Croats* and, first and foremost *Serbs,* supported by the fanatical *Slavic Orthodox* church, slaughter Muslims in *Bosnia*. More than 200,000 Muslims died during this bloody conflict, primarily at the hands of *Serbs*, before the West finally intervened to stop the bloodshed. What makes this example especially repugnant is the fact that the West committed the crime of enforcing a strict arms embargo against defenseless *Bosnian* Muslims who were fighting well-armed *Serb* forces. These murderous Serbs were filled with rage in their hearts against Islam. When the slaughter finally reached a certain acceptable, or unacceptable if you will, level of Muslim eradication, the West intervened by bombing *Serbia*. Recently, some in the West reminded Muslims of this "favor." However, what the West should have done is let Muslims raise arms and defend themselves, rather than deprive them of weapons and force them to await this "generous favor," which came after years of passiveness during which Muslims were

---

[18] Lewis, "The Roots of Muslim Rage."

being slaughtered by the tens of thousands every year. Yet ironically, they call Islam, "violent." This is the "latest experience" Muslims had with Christianity.[19]

It was also a war in which many of today's Al-Qa'ida members, and other jihadists, fought.

The theme of the "inviolability of sacred Muslim land" is one that is central to Al-Qa'ida's message, be it the "occupation" of Saudi Arabia, and now that the U.S. is drawing down in Saudi Arabia, of the entire Saudi peninsula. Israel's existence on "Arab land" is also cited as a cause for Jihad. This is also a modern phenomenon, with no basis in Muslim history. It is more properly linked to a misuse of Muslim custom to legitimize a reaction to a sense of inferiority, exemplified by the necessity of support from the U.S. to provide regional security, and their inability to defeat the Jewish state. The "Islamic myth" of the sacredness of all Muslim land, now taught to several generations, has become its own reality. The borders of Islam, although in the early period generally greatly expanding, did not always do so. "Adjustments" to those borders based on military necessity were not viewed as grave setbacks to the religion. In fact, today's hyper-reaction by Islamists to any border changes represents a lack of faith in the ultimate victory of Islam that was not shared by Islam's early jihadists. Juxtaposing the Islamic reaction to the Crusades with their reaction to the creation of the State of Israel is an interesting case in point. One would think that Islam, in a prolonged struggle with Christianity, and facing a religion that also had universalist aspirations, would have viewed the establishment of the Crusader Kingdom in an area that greatly exceeds that of the current state of Israel, as a greater threat than the modern Jewish state. There was, however, never a continuous state of combat against the Crusader Kingdoms, and in fact Muslim rulers at times made alliances with the Crusaders.

> The capture of Jerusalem by the Crusaders in 1099 C.E. was a triumph of Christendom and a disaster for the Muslims and also for the Jews in the city. To judge by the Arabic historiography of the period, it aroused very little interest in the region. Appeals by the local Muslims to Damascus and Baghdad for help remained unanswered, and the newly established Crusader principalities from Antioch to Jerusalem soon fitted into the game of Levantine politics, with cross-religious alliances in a pattern of rivalries between and among Muslim and Christian princes.[20] ... [T]he Crusades, ...had aroused remarkably little concern at the time they occurred. The vast and rich Arabic historiography of the period duly records the Crusaders' arrival, their battles, and the states that they established but shows little or no awareness of the nature and purposes of the venture....Awareness of the Crusades as a distinctive historical phenomenon dates from the nineteenth century, and the translation of European books on history. Since then, there is a new perception of the Crusades as an early prototype of the expansion of European imperialism into the Islamic world. A more accurate description would present them as a long-delayed, very limited, and finally

---

[19] Abualrub, *Holy War Crusades Jihad: In the Torah, the Gospels, and the Quran*, 214.
[20] Bernard Lewis, *The Crisis of Islam* (New York: The Modern Library, 2003), 47.

ineffectual response to the Jihad.[21] In the fifteenth century, the Christian counterattack expanded. The Tatars were expelled from Russia, and the Moors from Spain. But in southeastern Europe, where the Ottoman sultan confronted first the Byzantine and then the Holy Roman emperor, Muslim power prevailed, and these other setbacks were seen as minor and peripheral.[22]

Today, the only "victories" by the jihadists, and thus by Islam, are attained in Al-Qa'ida or Palestinian suicide attacks. Mass "education" has distorted history, and the information media inflame passions.

While modern jihadists can link the case for the removal of all non-Muslims from the Arabian Peninsula to Muhammad, insisting on an absolute ban distorts Muslim history and practice. "The classical Arabic historians tell us that in the year 20 of the Muslim era, corresponding to 641 C.E., the Caliph 'Umar decreed that Jews and Christians should be removed from all but the southern and eastern fringes of Arabia, in fulfillment of an injunction of the Prophet uttered on his deathbed: 'Let there not be two religions in Arabia.'....'Umar's decree was both limited and compassionate. It did not include southern and southeastern Arabia, not seen as part of the Islamic Holy Land."[23] U.S. presence in the Gulf States and, potentially in Yemen (especially the Yemeni island of Socotra), is not a religious problem. U.S. power in the region is, however, a great threat to Al-Qa'ida and other jihadists.

> In recent years, there have been some changes of perception and, consequently, of tactics among Muslims. Some of them still see the West in general and its present leader the United States in particular as the ancient and irreconcilable enemy of Islam, the one serious obstacle to the restoration of God's faith and law at home and their ultimate universal triumph. There are others who, while remaining committed Muslims and well aware of the flaws of modern Western society, nevertheless also see its merits — its inquiring spirit, which produced modern science and technology; its concern for freedom, which created modern democratic government. These, while retaining their own beliefs and their own culture, seek to join us in reaching toward a freer and better world. There are some again who, while seeing the West as their ultimate enemy and as the source of all evil, are nevertheless aware of its power, and seek some temporary accommodation in order better to prepare for the final struggle. We would be wise not to confuse the second and the third.[24]

It is the responsibility of the Intelligence Community, armed with access to more operational details of the jihadists' actions, which transcend academic knowledge of Islam, Muslim history, culture (to include family, clan and tribal implications), and the theory of Jihad, to provide an understanding of and opportunities to exploit their centers of gravity. An intelligence analyst who is familiar with many of the above-mentioned academic perspectives, coupled with intelligence sources, is best positioned to make strategic threat assessments.

---

[21] Lewis, *The Crisis of Islam,* 50-51.

[22] Lewis, *The Crisis of Islam,* 51.

[23] Lewis, *The Crisis of Islam,* xxxi.

[24] Lewis, *The Crisis of Islam,* 28.

The Intelligence Community, acting in concert with the law enforcement community, must, of course, also undertake operational and tactical analysis in support of "counterterror" operations. This analysis, however, must occur within the framework of the day-to-day struggle to contain and destroy "terrorists"; the U.S. must develop a mechanism to understand and attack the jihadists' strategic centers of gravity. This "mechanism" should exist within the Intelligence Community today, as it did during the Cold War. The expertise to get the Community to that level will not be built in a short time.

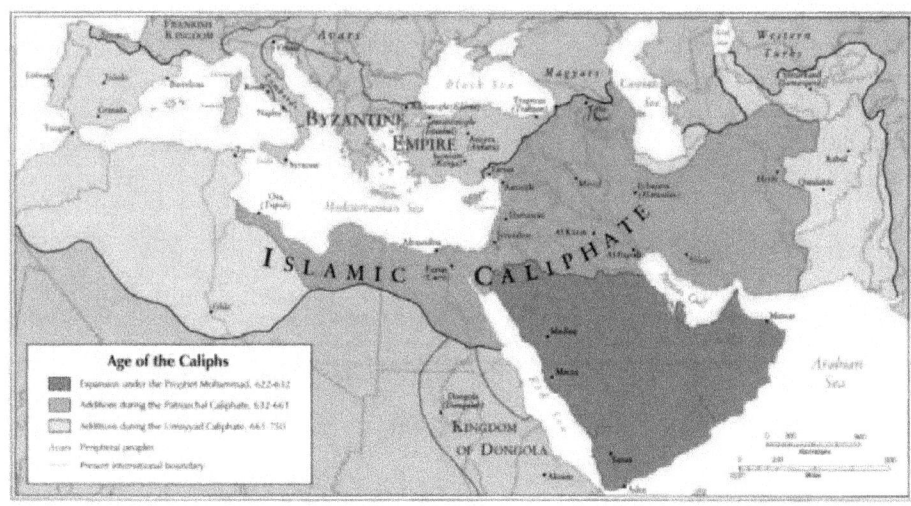

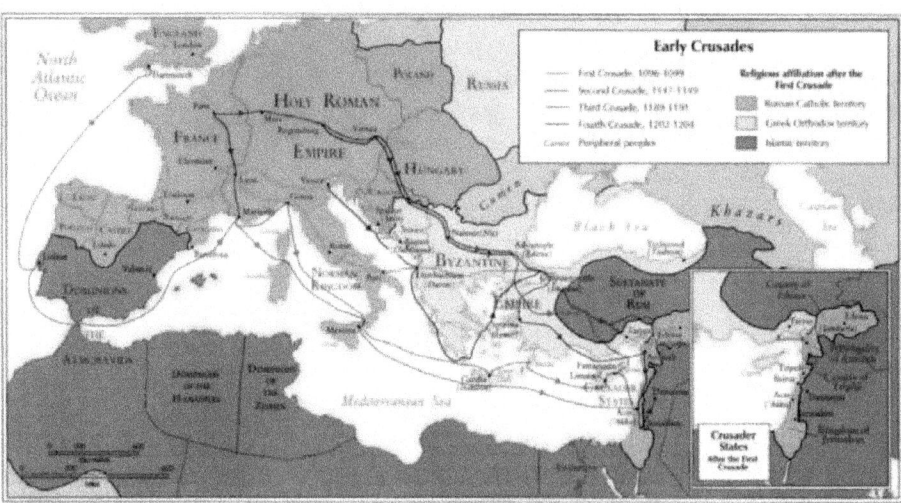

Figure 1. (U) Source: CIA, Atlas of the Middle East, 1993, 7.

Historical Eras for figure 1

BC	**3500-1100** Sumerians develop writing . . . first cereal agriculturists . . . bronze discovered . . . Upper and Lower Egypt united . . . Pharaonic Age begins
	1225 Moses leads Jews out of Egypt
	994 David captures Jerusalem . . . creates Jewish state of Israel
	63 Roman Legion seizes Jerusalem
AD	**0** Birth of Jesus . . . founder of Christianity
	70 Romans raze Jewish temple in Jerusalem
	330 Constantine moves capital of Roman Empire to Constantinople
	570-632 Life of Muhammad . . . founder of Islam
	622 The Hegira . . . Muhammad's flight from Mecca to Medina . . . year 1 in Islamic calendar
Age of the Caliphs	**632-661** Period of Patriarchal Caliphate . . . Caliph elected by Muhammad's original followers . . . realm includes Egypt and Mesopotamia
	656 Islamic schism between Sunnis and Shias begins with murder of Caliph Othman
	661-750 Umayyad Caliphate . . . first Islamic dynasty . . . Muslim Empire reaches greatest extent . . . centered in Damascus
	750 Marwan II first Caliph not recognized by all of Islamic world . . . end of Age of the Caliphs
	750-1258 Abbasids end Umayyad rule and create new dynasty . . . Baghdad becomes capital
	760 Tartar tribe from Armenia develops Turkish Empire
Early Crusades	**1096-1099** First Crusade captures Edessa, Antioch, and Jerusalem . . . creates Crusader States
	1147-1149 Second Crusade launched with loss of Edessa to Muslims
	1189-1191 Third Crusade initiated with loss of Jerusalem to Muslims . . . fails to retake the city
	1202-1204 Fourth Crusade intended against Muslim Egypt . . . redirected toward Greek Constantinople . . . sacks Constantinople and creates Latin Empire

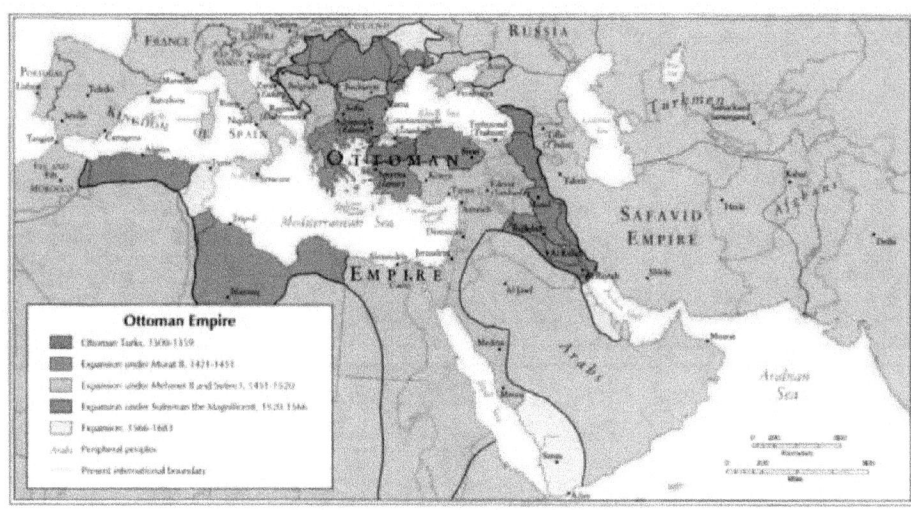

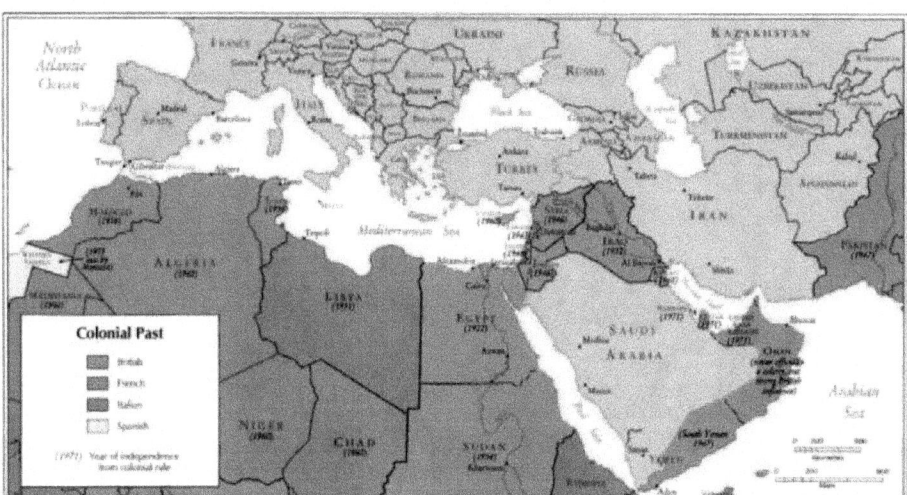

Figure 2. (U) Source: CIA, Atlas of the Middle East, 1993, 7.

Key For Figure 2

AD	**1219** Genghis Khan devastates eastern Persia **1228-1229** Fifth Crusade results in Christian control of Jerusalem **1291** Last Crusader state falls to Mamluk Empire
Ottoman Empire	**1453** Constantinople captured by Mehmet II . . . becomes capital of Ottoman Empire . . . end of Byzantine Empire **1514-1517** Sultan Selim I conquers Anatolia, Syria, the Levant, and Egypt . . . greatest Ottoman advance into Europe **1602-1627** War between Ottoman Empire and Persia **1683** Ottoman Empire reaches its greatest extent
	1760 Mamluks regain Egypt **1798-1801** Napolean invades Egypt . . . advances into Syria . . . Ottoman Turks defeated
Colonial Past	**1831-1839** Egyptian occupation of Syria . . . British seize Aden in 1839 **1840** Mohammad Ali secures Egyptian independence from Ottoman Turks **1859-1869** Excavation of Suez Canal **1860** French Army stops Druze massacre of Christians . . . charter guarantees Christian rule of Lebanon **1882** British occupy Egypt to suppress civil war . . . Britain appoints a Consul General in Cairo **1900** Germans and Ottoman Turks begin construction of Hejaz Railway **1920** France rules Syria and Lebanon and Britain rules Iraq and Palestine through League of Nations mandates

THE ROAD TO PARADISE:
JIHAD-MARTYRDOM-PARADISE

"So he [the Old Man of the Mountain — leader of the Assassin Ismaeli sect of Shi'a Islam] had fashioned it [his gardens] after the description that Mohommet [Muhammad] gave of his Paradise, to wit, that it should be a beautiful garden running with conduits of wine and milk and honey and water, and full of lovely women for the delectation of all its inmates."[25] It is for his place in the afterlife that a Muslim lives. Juxtaposed with Paradise is a vivid description of hell in which a Muslim may also spend eternity. Modern jihadists are obsessed with going to Paradise. This leads them to a formula "guaranteed" to gain admission. "It is true that the promise of paradise is given to every believer who performs the five basic duties [five pillars of Islam will be described later], but none of them would enable him to gain paradise as surely as participation in Jihad."[26] The leaders of Al-Qa'ida, and other jihadist groups, by definition, seek to participate in Jihad. They, however, seek victory, and not necessarily martyrdom. They do, however, accept martyrdom in the conduct of their Jihad. The formula that they sell their followers is a simple one: Jihad-martyrdom-paradise. They look for what they call "the young men," and now "the young women," to conduct "martyrdom operations." Fundamental to achieving paradise, therefore, is participation in a Jihad. This has led many jihadists to "follow Jihad." Many have fought in multiple locations, to include: Afghanistan (against the Soviets, Northern Alliance, US/Karzai government); Tajikistan; Bosnia; Chechnya; Kashmir; Uzbekistan; internal to their home countries (Algeria, Egypt), and more. Although participation in a Jihad was a simpler proposition under Mohammad, not long after his death it began to become complex. Laws of Jihad have changed through the centuries as Islam came to grips with changing circumstances. (This was even true under Mohammad). Modern Jihad, following the fall of the Ottoman Empire and the end of the Caliphate, makes the certainty of a "proper" Jihad more nebulous. A full understanding of the rules and circumstances of Jihad is necessary to see why the jihadists have a vulnerable, strategic center of gravity on this issue.

Jihad is fundamental to Islam. Without the concept of Jihad, Islam would not only be a much different religion, it probably would not have survived to emerge from Medina. In fact the several "offshoots" of Islam that exclude Jihad (Maziyariyya[27], Ahmadiya[28], Baha'i[29]) are persecuted by the Muslim community as heretical, and the Baha'i rightfully consider themselves a separate religion. "It is well known that there are five points that in

---

[25] Bernard Lewis, *The Assassins: A Radical Sect in Islam,* paperback edition (New York: Basic Books, 2003), 7.

[26] Khadduri, *War and Peace in the Law of Islam,* 62.

[27] Khadduri, *War and Peace in the Law of Islam,* 60.

[28] Ignaz Goldziher, *Introduction to Islamic Theology and Law,* trans. Andras and Ruth Hamori (Princeton, NJ: Princeton University Press, 1981), 264.

[29] William S. Hatcher and J. Douglass Martin, *The Baha'I Faith: The Emerging Global Religion* (San Francisco: Harper and Row, Publishers, 1984), 13.

their fully developed form serve as the foundation pillars of the Muslim religion. Their first outlines — the liturgical and humanitarian ones — began to appear in the Meccan period, but they received fixed form only in Medina. The five are: 1) the profession of faith in the one God, and the acknowledgment that Muhammad is the messenger of God; 2) the ritual of the prayer service (which began in the form of vigils and recitations that show a link to the traditions of eastern Christianity, as do such accompanying features as genuflection, prostration, and preliminary washing); 3) alms, which had originally been a matter of voluntary charity, but later became a contribution payable in fixed amounts toward the needs of the community; 4) fasting, originally on the tenth day of the first month (in imitation of the Jewish Day of Atonement, 'ashura), later during Ramadan, the ninth month of the lunar calendar; 5) pilgrimage to the Ka'ba, the house of God, the old Arab national sanctuary in Mecca."[30] Some have called "Jihad" a sixth pillar of the faith. In fact, one of the Islamic schools of legal theory, the Khariji, includes Jihad among the five pillars (not as a sixth pillar but as part of the five, an iman [a necessity]).[31]

The term Jihad has been often, and deliberately, misused. It does not translate well into the supposed "Western" equivalent of Crusade, nor is it a "holy war." These translations serve as "shorthand" to be used superficially, but not when a deep understanding is necessary. "The term Jihad is derived from the verb jahada (abstract noun, juhd) which means 'exerted'; its juridical-theological meaning is exertion of one's power in Allah's path, that is, the spread of the belief in Allah and in making His word supreme over this world. The individual's recompense would be the achievement of salvation, since the Jihad is Allah's direct way to paradise."[32]

> The importance of the Jihad in Islam lay in shifting the focus of attention of the [Arab] tribes from their intertribal warfare to the outside world; Islam outlawed all forms of war except the Jihad, that is, the war in Allah's path. It would, indeed, have been difficult for the Islamic state to survive had it not been for the doctrine of Jihad, replacing tribal raids, and directing the enormous energy of the tribes from an inevitable internal conflict to unite and fight against the outside world in the name of the new faith.[33]

Today, Jihad, and the aspects of Islam directed against an external enemy, is a powerful force to rally the faithful. To a Muslim world divided and under tremendous pressure to come to terms with the modern world, dominated by Western concepts that are both alien and threatening to the traditional fabric of Muslim life, Jihad can appear to be an answer.

There are theoretical aspects of "Jihad" that have evolved in Islam to define the concept in other than militaristic terms. These aspects, or rather redefinitions, are currently mostly used to obfuscate and deflect criticism from those Muslim leaders that are calling for Jihad. When Yasser Arafat, Saddam Hussein, or Usama bin Laden call for Jihad, they

---

[30] Goldziher, *Introduction to Islamic Theology and Law*, 13-15.
[31] Khadduri, *War and Peace in the Law of Islam*, 60.
[32] Khadduri, *War and Peace in the Law of Islam*, 55.
[33] Khadduri, *War and Peace in the Law of Islam*, 62.

are calling for an armed struggle. When religious opinions (fatwas) are issued legitimizing Jihad, they are supporting armed action. It is important to understand other potential meanings of Jihad within Islamic jurisprudence, especially when seeking to influence an Islamic "reformation." It is vital, from a threat perspective, not to be confused by what is meant when Jihad is invoked.

> Some modern Muslims, particularly when addressing the outside world, explain the duty of Jihad in a spiritual and moral sense. The overwhelming majority of early authorities, citing the relevant passages in the Qur'an, the commentaries, and the traditions of the Prophet, discuss Jihad in military terms....For most of the fourteen centuries of recorded Muslim history, Jihad was most commonly interpreted to mean armed struggle for the defense or advancement of Muslim power.[34]

There are circumstances, however, in which the term Jihad, in fact, does mean other than military "striving" or "exertion." This less-used concept can best be explained by looking at the duality by which Islam views the world. "Islamic geography divides the world into seven climatic zones, but there is a more trenchant division: the land of Islam [dar al-Islam] and the land of war [dar al-Harb]. The second category includes regions among whose inhabitants unbelief still rules although the summons (da'wa) to embrace Islam has been carried to them. It is the duty of the head of the Islamic state to levy war on such territories. That is Jihad, the holy war ordered in the Qur'an, one of the surest paths to martyrdom."[35]

> The Jihad, in the broad sense of exertion, does not necessarily mean war or fighting, since exertion in Allah's path may be achieved by peaceful as well as violent means....The jurists, however, have distinguished four different ways in which the believer may fulfill his Jihad obligation: by his heart; his tongue; his hands; and by the sword. The first is concerned with combating the devil and in the attempt to escape his persuasion to evil. This type of Jihad, so significant in the eyes of the Prophet Muhammad, was regarded as the greater Jihad. The second and third are mainly fulfilled in supporting the right and correcting the wrong. The fourth is precisely equivalent to the meaning of war, and is concerned with fighting the unbelievers and the enemies of the faith. The believers are under the obligation of sacrificing their "wealth and lives" in the prosecution of war.[36]

Within dar al-Islam, Jihad (with exceptions) has a peaceful meaning, in relations to dar al-Harb, Jihad is war.

Jihad, however, is not a static concept, but an adaptive one. What started out as warfare to expand the dar al-Islam, has evolved into the more expansive definition of "fighting the

---

[34] Lewis, *The Crisis of Islam,* 30-31.
[35] Goldziher, *Introduction to Islamic Theology and Law,* 102.
[36] Khadduri, *War and Peace in the Law of Islam,* 56-57.

unbelievers and the enemies of the faith." "The Jihad, in other words is a sanction against polytheism and must be suffered by all non-Muslims who reject Islam, or in the case of the dhimmis (scriptuaries), refuse to pay the poll tax....it is also a form of punishment to be inflicted upon Islam's enemies and the renegades from the faith."[37] This explains the centuries of warfare (defined as Jihad) between what westerners consider Muslims. "According to Islamic law, it is lawful to wage war against four types of enemies: infidels, apostates, rebels, and bandits. Although all four types of wars are legitimate, only the first two count as Jihad."[38] Thus, in the dar al-Islam, for Jihad, rebels must be classified as apostates.

> The apostate, *murtadd*, is one who had been or had become a Muslim, and then had abandoned Islam and adopted another faith or, more commonly, reverted to his previous or ancestral faith.... The question of a war against apostasy arose on the death of the Prophet, when a number of Arabian tribes refused to transfer to the newly appointed Caliph the allegiance and tribute which they had agreed to give to the Prophet....The ensuing wars, by which they were forcibly brought back to their allegiance, are known in Muslim annals as the Wars of the *Ridda* or Apostasy....Apostasy is extremely rare in Islamic history, and the apostasy of regimes or countries even rarer. Accusations of apostasy, however, are not uncommon.[39]

> The rules of warfare against the apostate are very much harsher than those governing warfare against the unbeliever. He may not be given quarter or safe conduct, and no truce or agreement with him is permissible. If captured, he is not a prisoner of war. He cannot become a dhimmi, nor can he hope, like other captives of Jihad, to live on as a slave. The only options before him are recantation or death.[40]

The necessity for jihadists to characterize those Muslims who disagree with them as apostates explains the vehemence of the hatred exhibited by the jihadists toward those Muslims who do not share their views. This hatred is evidenced even against learned Islamic jurists who refuse to issue, or do not support, a jihadist-requested fatwa. Jihadist leaders, although generally not learned enough themselves to qualify to issue a fatwa (including Usama bin Laden), have no tolerance for the learned jurists who argue against them.

Jihadists who call for Jihad against Muslim states must also so designate the rulers and state structures as apostate. There have been two periods in Islamic history, including today, wherein states are being seriously charged with apostasy.

> Both of them are periods when the Islamic heartlands of the Middle East were dominated and profoundly influenced by foreign, that is to say, non-Islamic,

---

[37] Khadduri, *War and Peace in the Law of Islam*, 59.

[38] Lewis, *The Crisis of Islam*, 31.

[39] Lewis, *The Political Language of Islam*, 84-85.

[40] Lewis, *The Political Language of Islam*, 85.

conquerors, and when a governing class emerged which professed Islam, but which followed many of the ways and customs of the former infidel masters.... The Mongols who conquered the Middle East in the thirteenth century brought with them the *Yasa*, the laws of Jenghiz Khan, and the social and political usages of the steppe peoples.... The question arose again in modern times, with the appearance, first in the Ottoman Empire and then in many Muslim states, of reformers and modernizers, who tried to introduce Western notions and practices and thereby, intentionally or unintentionally, to transform Muslim government and society. Many of their proposed changes were contrary to the shari'a [sacred Islamic law] as practiced and understood, and were bitterly opposed by sections of the ulema [professional men of religion], though supported by other groups. The reformers tried to deal with this problem in various ways, first by seeking to reinterpret shari'a, and when this failed to secure acceptance, to circumvent and ultimately to replace it with legal codes copied or adapted from European models....Some of the ulema, following an old established tradition of pliancy and conformism, were willing to accept and justify the action of sovereigns and ministers in this as in other matters. Other ulema, following an equally ancient tradition of rigorism and dissent, refused, and denounced these reforms as a betrayal of Islam and an attempt to lead the Muslim community from righteousness to sin."[41]

Obviously, today's jihadists agree with the latter opinion. Thus, the insistence on the removal of governments that refuse to institute shari'a.

As stated earlier, the rules of Jihad are adaptive. Although they are based on historical example, those examples are themselves expediencies of their times. The treatment of Arab tribes as apostates following the death of Muhammed is illustrative. Also interesting was an instance when the question of the permissibility of fighting fellow Muslims was decided, quite literally, on the battlefield. In 1107 the Seljuk Sultanate attempted to rid itself of the Ismaeli sect. The Ismaelis, hard pressed in their castle, started a religious controversy.

[The] Ismaelis claimed that they were good Muslims, believers in God and the Prophet, observers of the Holy Law. They differed from the Sunnis only concerning the Imamante [who should rule the Muslims], and it would therefore be proper for the Sultan to grant them a truce and terms, and accept their allegiance. This initiated a religious debate between the attackers and the defenders, and between different schools of thought in the attacking camp. Many of the Sultan's theological advisers were willing to accept the Ismaeli argument, but a few stood firm for a more rigorous attitude. "Let them answer this question," said one of them. "If your Imam were to permit you what the Holy Law forbids, and forbid you what the Holy Law permits, would you obey him? If they answer yes, their blood is lawful." Thanks to the insistence of the rigorists, the debate came to nothing and the siege continued.[42]

---

[41] Lewis, *The Political Language of Islam*, 86-88.

Fundamental to the Jihad-martyrdom-paradise paradigm is the "correctness" of the Jihad. If there is doubt as to the legitimacy of the Jihad, then death in the conduct of that Jihad is not martyrdom, and thus, a martyr's place in paradise is not assured. In fact, the opposite may be the case. By participating in a "false Jihad" the "jihadist" may be doomed to damnation. This represents a fundamental strategic center of gravity. It requires, however, a shift in Muslim public opinion to cast doubt on bin Laden's call for Jihad. This shift must be precipitated by a long and continuous denunciation of Al-Qa'ida by the learned jurists of Islam. This is not occurring. Modern Islamic jurists tend not to want to shape public perceptions. It is the rare jurist who will buck popular opinion, most preferring to view Al-Qa'ida, and other jihadist movements as political and not religious. A very strange thing for Islam, which by its nature can't separate the two.

> In classical Islam there is no distinction between Church and state.... At the present time, the very notion of a secular jurisdiction and authority — of a so-to-speak unsanctified part of life that lies outside the scope of religious law and those who uphold it — is seen as an impiety, indeed as the ultimate betrayal of Islam. The righting of this wrong is the principal aim of Islamic revolutionaries and, in general, of those described as Islamic fundamentalists.[43]

Traditional jurists, moreover, are at a disadvantage, as they find it difficult to argue that the "revolutionaries" are wrong.

Islamic jurists, the vast majority of whom disagree with Al-Qa'ida's methods and the correctness of the bin Laden Jihad, remain largely mute on the issue. Perhaps they are willing to allow the end, the creation of a world governed by shari'a, to justify the means used by the jihadists. Should they speak out in large numbers, it would put tremendous pressure on the jihadists to justify their continued widespread support in the Muslim world. Consensus of the community sets a strong precedent in Islamic law. This consensus currently appears (to the jihadist recruits and supporters) to support Jihad. It is this perception that can be changed by a concerted and prolonged vocal opposition to the jihadists by the Islamic majority jurists. Conversely, if modern jihadist views are allowed to prevail there is a risk that they will become accepted as "orthodox."

> I must now turn to a momentous principle which, more than any other, characterizes the development of Islamic law, and which has furnished a means of smoothing over divisions that resulted from the development of separate schools of law. In the midst of theoretical uncertainty about matters of usage, this principle came to prevail among Muslim theologians, and, in its various applications, has prevailed ever since. It is expressed in a statement ascribed to the Prophet: "My community will never agree on error (dalala)".... This fundamental concept of Islamic orthodoxy is embodied in

---

[42] Lewis, *The Assassins: A Radical Sect in Islam*, 53-54.
[43] Lewis, The Political Language of Islam, 2-3.

the Arabic technical term *ijma*, "agreement,"....Ijma is the key to a grasp of the historical evolution of Islam in its political, theological, and legal aspects. Whatever is accepted by the entire Islamic community as true and correct must be regarded as true and correct. To turn one's back on the ijma is to leave the orthodox community.... We shall see that only the continued effectiveness of this principle, throughout the history of Islam, explains that certain religious phenomena gained the stamp of orthodoxy because they had gained general acceptance, although in theory they should have been censured as being contrary to Islam. They had become established in the consensus and therefore, regardless of grave theological scruples about them, at length had to be granted approval, and on occasion even accepted as obligatory."[44]

The discussion of Jihad has been from a Sunni perspective. Groups that can be identified as "jihadist," including Al-Qa'ida, are Sunni. This in no way means that there is no threat from Shi'a groups. The example of Lebanese Hizballah in using suicide "martyrdom" operations is the "inspiration" for Al-Qa'ida and Palestinian "martyrdom" operations. The Shi'a doctrine of Jihad differs from that of the Sunnis on a theoretical level. It must be noted, however, that these theoretical differences will not stop Sunni-Shi'a cooperation against the U.S. in specific instances.

Shi'a and Sunni do not generally differ on the laws of Jihad, once legitimately labeled. Shi'ism, however, at least in theory, has suspended offensive Jihad, pending the return of the "hidden" imam. Iran's Ayatollah Khomeini issued "keys to paradise" to the soldiers conducting infantry wave attacks against Iraqi armor and artillery during the 1980-88 Iran-Iraq war. This defensive Jihad to repel the Iraqi attack was thus considered qualification for martyrdom. Ayatollah Khomeini did, however, chart a new course for Iranian Shi'ism by establishing a theocracy in Iran. "The office of ayatollah is a creation of the nineteenth century; the rule of Khomeini and of his successor as 'supreme jurist' an innovation of the twentieth."[45] Given Shi'ism's allowance for a religious leader to speak in the name of the "hidden imam" of our time, or more drastically the return of the imam as the Mahdi (Messiah), the proper Shi'a leader could arise that would be allowed to alter the traditional stance on offensive Jihad, and declare one. Ayatollah Khomeini came close to achieving this status before his death. Had he lived longer, his impact on Iranian Shi'ism would certainly have been more profound.

Generally speaking, the Shi'a law of the Jihad is not different from the Sunni; but linking the special duty of prosecuting the Jihad with the doctrine of walaya (allegiance to the imam), the concept of Jihad assumed in Shi'ism a special doctrinal significance. In Shi'a legal theory, not only would the failure of a non-Muslim to believe in Allah justify waging a Jihad, but also the failure of a Muslim to obey the imam would make him liable for punishment by a

---

[44] Goldziher, *Introduction to Islamic Theology and Law*, 50-51.
[45] Lewis, *What Went Wrong*, 114.

Jihad. While to the Sunni the Jihad is a sure way to Heaven, a Jihad without an allegiance to the imam would not constitute an iman (a necessary requirement for salvation) in the Shi'a creed.[46]

The Jihad is regarded as one of the chief functions of the imamate.... The imam, as the infallible ruler, is the only one who can judge when the Jihad should be declared and under what circumstances it would be advisable not to go to war with the enemy. If the imam finds it necessary to come to terms with the enemy, he may do so; he may even deem it necessary to seek the support of non-Muslims (including polytheists) in order to avoid risking defeat. Under no circumstances, however, should the imam risk a Jihad if he considers the enemy too powerful for him to win a victory, namely, if the enemy is at least twice as powerful as the Muslims....since the duty of calling believers to battle is a matter in which an infallible judgment is necessary...only an imam is capable of fulfilling such a duty. Further, it is deemed impossible to combat evil during the absence of the imam; the Jihad, accordingly, is regarded as inconsequential. Thus in Shi'a legal theory, the Jihad has entered a dormant stage — it is in a state of suspension. In contrast to the Sunni doctrine which requires the revival of the dormant Jihad when Muslim power is regained, the resumption of the Jihad in the Shi'a doctrine would be dependent on the return of the imam from his ghayba (absence), in the capacity of a Mahdi, who will triumphantly combat evil and re-establish justice and righteousness.[47]

---

[46] Khadduri, *War and Peace in the Law of Islam*, 66.
[47] Khadduri, *War and Peace in the Law of Islam*, 66-67.

JIHAD: THE LEGAL ARGUMENTS

Should a Jihad be called against the United States? Can Al-Qa'ida declare such a Jihad? Is Usama bin Laden qualified to issue a fatwa? Can jihadists use force to overturn governments to establish shari'a? Are the methods used by the jihadists legitimate? These are the basic questions around which the religious argument is theoretically formed. It must be emphasized, however, that currently committed jihadists will not be swayed by the outcome of this debate. Supporters, potential recruits, and marginally committed jihadists may, in fact, be swayed by the legal arguments. The ability of jihadists to recruit "martyrs" will likewise be greatly affected.

Usama bin Laden has been careful to formulate his fatwas declaring Jihad against the U.S. as being in the defense of Islam. Although dismissed by the U.S., since the U.S. is not attacking Islam, this formulation is vital in the legal argument. Islam recognizes two forms of Jihad, offensive and defensive. The conditions for these different Jihads vary greatly. The differences provide bin Laden the "grey area" in Islamic law in which he operates. "The Jihad...unless the Muslim community is subjected to a sudden attack and therefore all believers, including women and children, are under the obligation to fight, is regarded by all jurists, with almost no exception, as a collective obligation of the whole Muslim community [enforced by the state].[48]

> The leader of the Muslims in the Jihad is the sovereign or ruler of the Muslim state. In classical times, this meant the Caliph; later it meant whatever sultan or amir was in charge. At a time when Islamic standards of legitimacy and of justice were being whittled down to accommodate the harsh realities of military power, the jurists were careful to insist that the obligation of Jihad survived every change of government or regime, and was owed to any ruler actually possessing the necessary power. According to a saying improbably ascribed to the Prophet: "Jihad is incumbent upon you under every amir, whether he be godly or wicked, and even if he commits major sins." In Jihad, the subject's normal duty of obedience becomes one of active armed support.[49]

Al-Qa'ida does not constitute a state, and therefore insists that theirs is a defensive Jihad based upon a U.S. attack. Even in this circumstance, however, it is far from certain that a prolonged Jihad, absent the call from the ruler of a sovereign Muslim state, is appropriate.

The concepts of offensive and defensive Jihad, however, are not totally clear in their application. There is no doubt that a defensive Jihad automatically exists when Islam is suddenly attacked. However, what if the attack is not sudden, but a prolonged conflict? It should then still be up to the Muslim ruler, as is the case with an offensive Jihad, to make the determination if a Jihad is in the best interests of the Muslims. This then is Usama bin

---

[48] Khadduri, *War and Peace in the Law of Islam,* 60.
[49] Lewis, *The Political Language of Islam,* 73

Laden's dilemma. He has declared a prolonged Jihad against the United States, which, whether or not Islam has been attacked, provides for plenty of opportunity for Muslim rulers to declare Jihad. Not one Muslim ruler has done so. Bin Laden must thus both discredit the Muslim rulers and rely on the fatwas (his own and religious leaders) to legitimize his Jihad against the United States. There seems to be a mistaken belief, even among Muslims, and perhaps influenced by the Khomeini revolution in Iran, that religious authorities can declare Jihad, which many often do. When one looks throughout history, Muslim religious leaders have given opinions to imams as to the proper course of action. That action is, however, taken by the Muslim ruler. The jihadists of the modern Jihad, having dismissed the legitimacy of Muslim rulers, have taken matters into their own hands. It is, however, very difficult in Sunni Islam to dismiss the ruler.

Jihadists dedicated to the overthrow of a Muslim ruler have an even tougher legal position than does Al-Qa'ida. It is one thing to declare a Jihad against a non-Muslim state, however appropriate or inappropriate; it is quite another to declare a Jihad against a Muslim state (with or without a "godly" Muslim ruler).

> The major problem [for the jihadists] is the domination of the Muslim lands, Egypt and elsewhere, by apostates and secularists who, while pretending to be Muslims, are in fact destroying Islam from within. In their view, the major crime of Sadat, as of the Shah in Iran, Saddam Hussein in Iraq, Assad in Syria, and before them Nasser in Egypt and Ataturk in Turkey, was the abrogation of the Holy Law of Islam and the paganizing of Islamic society by the introduction and imposition of laws and usages imported from the outside world.... This, they assert, is the ultimate crime against God and his Holy Law, for which the penalty is death. Rulers and regimes that have abandoned the Holy Law have thereby forfeited their legitimacy; they have become the enemies of God and therefore of all good Muslims. The duty of Jihad...is incumbent upon all Muslims, but the first task is to destroy the tyrant at home and thus make possible the restoration of a truly Islamic society governed by Islamic law. After that, with God's help, the removal of the external enemy, whose penetration had been made possible by Muslim sinfulness and weakness, would be a relatively simple matter.[50]

This is where bin Laden and other jihadists differ on strategy. Bin Laden has opted to declare Jihad against the U.S. prior to overthrowing Muslim governments. Most jihadist groups focus on a particular country.

The "qualifications" to be a recognized ruler in Islam, and now that Islam is divided into modern countries, of a Muslim state, quickly succumbed to realpolitik following the death of Muhammed. What constitutes legitimacy has dwindled over the centuries. Today it can be summed up as "he who rules is legitimate."

---

[50] Lewis, *Islam in History*, 379.

In principle, a Muslim ruler who does not possess the necessary qualifications or who is not chosen or appointed according to the law, is a usurper. Among the Shi'a this remained a crucial question, and all Sunni rulers, not being of the line of Ali and not being nominated and appointed by an Alid predecessor, are usurpers. Among Sunni Muslims...effective power became a sufficient qualification. In a phrase used by the Maliki jurists of North Africa, "whose power prevails must be obeyed." The ruler need no longer be of the Prophet's tribe of Quraysh, as required by most legal formulations. He need no longer possess the legally prescribed qualifications of rectitude, judgment, physical soundness, wisdom, and courage. It is sufficient if he can stay in power and keep order."[51]

"Only the Khawary [Kharijis], it seems, had openly advocated the principle of revolution. To them the Caliphate was a purely democratic institution...which empowers the electorate to depose or put to death a Caliph who violated his duties."[52] In fact, Usama bin Laden is accused of being (or acting like) a Khawary.

The jurists, in their arguments against rebellion repeated again and again that tyranny and impiousness is better than anarchy.[53] Even...in times of decadence, when pious Muslim authors saw the body politic as diseased and the service of the state as a contamination, they held firm to the principle that the authority of the Muslim ruler, however obtained and exercised, was a divinely ordained necessity....[54]

Muslim rulers who are currently targeted by the jihadists meet this rather simple criteria (especially if they are not faced with a jihadist insurrection).

The debate, however, was never finalized. While the reality has been that a Muslim ruler is legitimate by virtue of his capability to rule, the theory of legitimacy is problematic.

Religious writers take a less lenient, or perhaps one should say less pragmatic, view of repressive government. They are more insistent in reminding the ruler of the worldly limits of his power, more explicit in asserting that obedience has its limits....If the ruler commands something which is contrary to God's law, the subject's duty of obedience lapses. Some go even further and assert what amounts to a right, or even a duty, of disobedience. The definition of this right or duty, and the determining point at which it comes into operation, constitute one of the most fundamental problems of Islamic political thought and life.[55]

---

[51] Lewis, *The Political Language of Islam*, 102.
[52] Khadduri, *War and Peace in the Law of Islam*, 12.
[53] Khadduri, *War and Peace in the Law of Islam*, 13.
[54] Lewis, *The Political Language of Islam*, 26.
[55] Lewis, *The Political Language of Islam,* 70.

This problem is at the heart of Muslim government's battles against Islamists. The governments claim Islamic legitimacy. The Islamists view their obligation of obedience to have lapsed without the imposition of strict Shari'a law; the jihadists view it as their duty to remove such a government. "This [the replacement of shari'a law by other laws not divine in origin], from the traditionalist point of view, is the ultimate betrayal, the worst of all disasters, worse even than infidel conquest and rule, since, under a semblance of Islam, it seeks to subvert the loyalty of the Muslims and destroy the faith and law by which they live. Those who impose infidel laws are infidels; if they claim to be Muslims, then they are apostates, and must be treated as such."[56] Even in that case, however, Islam has come to terms with the realities of power.

> In time the duty of disobedience was hedged around with restrictions and qualifications and was in effect forgotten in the general acceptance, in theory as well as in practice, of the most complete quietism. A fourteenth century *qadi* [judge], al-Iji, still mentions, somewhat obliquely, the duty of resistance to sin; it only applies, however, if two conditions are met. First, a man must be satisfied that his action will not stir up sedition (*thawaran fitna*) and that it will achieve its purpose. (If he thinks that it will not achieve its purpose, then resistance is meritorious, but not obligatory.) Second, there must be no snooping (*tajassus*). In other words, don't go looking for trouble; if you meet it try to avoid it; and do not resist until success is a foregone conclusion.[57]

Based upon his "world view," Usama bin Laden obviously believes that he can both overthrow the Saudi regime, and successfully conduct Jihad against the United States.

To Al-Qa'ida there is another and perhaps greater shortcoming of today's Muslim ruler: They refuse to assume their responsibility of leading the Jihad, and have cooperated with the enemies of Islam. Thus, Muslim rulers assert their authority to declare, or not declare, a Jihad, and jihadists refuse to recognize their authority because the rulers, especially according to Al-Qa'ida, are obligated to do so.

The question of whether the United States is a legitimate subject of a Jihad is complex. There is no doubt that the U.S. is not an Islamic country, and therefore, is in the dar al-Harb. There is also no doubt that the U.S. government knows of Islam and could have accepted the Prophet. On a simple level, it would therefore be incumbent upon a Muslim ruler to declare a Jihad against the U.S. and give its people a choice between Islam and the status of dhimmi (paying the pole tax). It was recognized, even by Muhammed, that such a rigid application of Jihad would have doomed Islam. Thus, accommodations have always been made to practical considerations of political and military realities. This is why the Islamic ruler is left with the ultimate decision on offensive Jihad. It is also why a

---

[56] Lewis, *The Political Language of Islam*, 87.
[57] Lewis, *Islam in History*, 314-315.

third "house" has been created between dar al-Islam and dar al-Harb, the dar al-Ahd (territory in treaty relation with Islam) or dar al-Sulh (territory at peace with Islam).[58]

The earliest accommodation to Jihad was made by Muhammad prior to his ascendancy in Mecca.

> In the early spring of 628 Muhammad felt strong enough to attempt an attack on Mecca. On the way, however, it became clear that the attempt was premature and the expedition was converted into a peaceful pilgrimage. The Muslim leaders met Meccan negotiators at a place called Hudaybiyya, on the borders of the sacred territory around Mecca, in which, according to pre-Islamic usage, no fighting could take place during certain periods of the year. The negotiations ended in a ten-year truce [which actually only lasted three or four years] and the Muslims were given the right to perform the pilgrimage to Mecca in the following year and to stay there for three days. In later times, the agreement at Hudaybiyya served as the prophetic precedent to determine the Shari'a rules governing the interruption of the Jihad for negotiation and truce.[59]

A more telling precedent was set with the Christian country of Ethiopia.

> Ethiopia enjoyed a unique position in the eyes of the Muslims and may be regarded as the classic example of a non-Muslim state which Islam voluntarily declared to be immune from the Jihad. In formulating their opinions, Muslim publicists were primarily guided by the traditional reports about Islam's early relations with Ethiopia [Ethiopia provided safe-haven to some of Muhammad's followers, and recognized Muhammad as a prophet] as well as by the fact that Ethiopia remained for centuries untouched by Muslim forces."[60]

This position of Ethiopia, and later Nubia, creates another theoretical status between dar al-Islam and dar al-Harb, the dar al-Hiyad (world of neutrality).

> While some jurists recognized a third division of the world, called dar al-Ahd or dar al-Sulh, comprising countries in treaty relations with Islam, most of them considered this division as part either of the dar al-Islam or dar al-Harb. No jurist, however, would approve of a country being allowed to choose without Islam's consent an intermediary status between dar al-Islam and dar al-Harb....If in principle the concept of neutrality has no place in the Muslim jural order, the law, however, was not enforced without regard to certain exceptional cases for doctrinal no less than for practical considerations. Islam voluntarily refrained from attacking certain territories which

---

[58] Khadduri, *War and Peace in the Law of Islam*, 208.

[59] Bernard Lewis, *The Arabs in History*, 6th ed. (New York: Oxford University Press), 42-43.

[60] Khadduri, *War and Peace in the Law of Islam*, 253.

were regarded, whether in deference to their benevolent attitude toward the Prophet Muhammad and his companions or because of their inaccessibility, as immune from the Jihad. Such territories, constituting a separate division of the world, may be called — following the pattern of dividing the world into dars — dar al-Hiyad or the world of neutrality.... The world of neutrality, however, is not a self-constituting division of the world, for under the legal system which regards all countries as inherently hostile save those which have obtained security by Islam's consent, only those states which Islam agreed to spare from the Jihad might be regarded as neutral...Neutralization, therefore, not neutrality, may be said to have been permissible in Muslim legal theory, and practice....[61]

The United States could theoretically be "neutralized" by Islam. Is there a basis, however, for doing this? It is obviously too late to follow the Ethiopian model of providing aid to Muhammad's companions and followers. It is doubtful that the U.S. government would take a position on the prophethood of Muhammad. The Nubian model may, therefore, be more applicable.

After an unsuccessful attempt to annex her, Nubia [approximately current day Sudan], unlike Ethiopia, forced Islam to respect her independence and establish reciprocal trade relations with her. After the occupation of Egypt by Amr ibn al-As, the encounters between Muslims and Nubians taught both the lesson that they could come to terms with each other and refrain from attacking the territory of one another. Thereupon, the new governor of Egypt, Abd-Allah ibn Abi Sarh, concluded a treaty (A.D. 652) by virtue of which the Nubians were to pay an annual tribute of 360 slaves with a quid pro quo of wheat, barley, horses, and clothing....The tribute, known as the *baqt*, was not in the form of *jizya* [poll tax], for neither had the Nubians become dhimmis nor was the annual payment a sign of submission. It was rather a reciprocal trade agreement.... The treaty, with no specified duration, obviously could not last more then ten years [the length of the Hudaybiyya treaty]; but since the payment of the baqt was annual, the two parties must have tacitly or overtly renewed the treaty from time to time. In practice it lasted for over six hundred years, until Fatimid rule in Egypt.... It follows therefore that in theory Islam took the view that Nubia was temporarily outside the bounds of the Jihad, although the period of exclusion lasted for six centuries...It may be argued that Nubia was dar al-Ahd, as it was in treaty relations with Islam; but since the nature of the treaty is such that it did not pay tribute to Islam for the maintenance of the peace (as in other tributary relations) but paid rather on a reciprocal basis, it follows that its position resembles in some respects that of Ethiopia, defined by the terms of the treaty which gave her a special status in Muslim law. This status, agreed upon by both parties to last for the duration of the treaty, is a qualified status of neutralization.[62]

---

[61] Khadduri, *War and Peace in the Law of Islam*, 252.

While the exact length of a permissible treaty was a matter of debate, Islam learned very early in its history that constant Jihad could spell a death sentence for the religion. Therefore, accommodation was recognized as necessary when the relative strength of Islam and its adversary was so lopsided as to make victory unlikely. This, of course, was in direct contradiction to a belief in Allah's help that would overcome all odds. Islam, however, accommodated itself to the reality of overwhelming force arrayed against it.

> In the early days there seemed to be no reason to doubt that the extension of Islam to all the world belonged to a near rather than a distant future. With breathtaking speed, the Arab Muslim armies advanced out of Arabia, westwards to the Atlantic and the Pyrenees, eastwards to India and China. They had overcome the two greatest empires of the time, in Persia and Byzantium.... Some utterances at the time clearly reflect the belief that the God-given task of bringing Islam to all the world would soon be completed....By the early ninth century, Muslims began to realize that this fulfillment was not imminent, and in popular religion and legend it was postponed to a remote, indeed a messianic, future. With this realization came important changes in the Muslim perception of the frontier, and of the nature and conduct of relations with the powers that existed on the other side.[63]

Thus, although any country could be allowed to be "neutralized," the question is when it is proper to do so. This decision, although framed by religious precedent and guidelines, is left to the legitimate ruler. "...the duration of the treaties with non-Muslim authorities was specified by Muslim jurists. The Hanafi and Shafi'I schools held that a peace treaty with the enemy should not exceed a period of ten years. They based their argument on the Hudaybiyya treaty...which stipulated that the period of peace would last for ten years. Certain jurists maintained that the Hudaybiyya peace did not last ten years; they, accordingly, tolerated no peace treaty for a period exceeding three or four years."[64] Interestingly the jurist school associated with the current Wahhabi sect presented an early, contrary opinion. "Other jurists like the Hanbali jurist al-Hajjawi, advised the imam to conclude a peace treaty for more than ten years if the Muslims were weak and unable to resume the war with the enemy."[65]

Weakness, however, is a relative term and often difficult to discern. In early Islam, the Arabs seemed unconcerned about challenging the two preeminent powers of their known world, Persia and Byzantium. "There was an almost unanimous belief on the part of the Muslims, based on a divine revelation to Muhammad, that they would successfully conquer Persian and Byzantine dominions."[66] Furthermore, the laws of Jihad allow for four options, the enemy will: adopt Islam; remain polytheists and forfeit property and possibly

---

[62] Khadduri, *War and Peace in the Law of Islam*, 259-61.
[63] Lewis, *The Political Language of Islam*, 75.
[64] Khadduri, *War and Peace in the Law of Islam*, 219.
[65] Khadduri, *War and Peace in the Law of Islam*, 220.
[66] Khadduri, *War and Peace in the Law of Islam*, 100.

lives; pay tribute by virtue of a peace treaty; be given safe conduct. They do not envision a Muslim defeat as a potential outcome.

> In his Kitab al-Ahkam al-Sultaniyya, Mawardi advises the imam never to give up his fight with the enemy until victory is achieved.... Mawardi, however, is silent about an unsuccessful war with the enemy, and to him, as well as to many other jurists, the possibility of a defeat is dismissed as if entirely non-existent.... Some jurists, however, argued that if a catastrophe had befallen the Muslims (qualifying their remark by *istaghfir Allah*, God forbid) the imam might come to terms with the enemy for a period not exceeding the terms of the Hudaybiyya treaty, on the grounds of force *majeur*, provided that the Muslims should resume the Jihad after the expiration of the treaty if the imam decided that he was able to do so. If the imam feels that the Muslims are not powerful enough to resume the fighting, he may renew the truce for a similar period — but not longer — for if he concluded a truce for a longer period, it would be null and void."[67]

The Nubian precedent of 600 years, of course, allows for great flexibility in treaty renewal.

The Qur'an is very explicit, in numbers, about the definition of relative strength. This definition later had to take into consideration qualitative and material differences, to approximate what the Soviets termed a "correlation of forces" analysis.

> On the basis of a Qur'anic injunction which stated that twenty believers can fight two hundred, later abrogated by another that one thousand believers can fight two thousand — for Allah "knows that there is a weakness amongst you" — some jurists concluded that the Muslims were to be relieved of fighting if their numerical strength were less than half that of their enemy. Other jurists maintained that the term "strength" should not be construed on strictly numerical grounds, but on the power of resistance and the equipment of the enemy....Ibn Hanbal permits retreat if the enemy's power exceeded twice that of the believers.... Awza'i goes further in elaborating this rule and argues that, if the imam feels weakness in his forces, or if the Muslims are engaged in a civil war, he might come to terms with the enemy even at the sacrifice of paying an annual tribute. In giving this opinion Awza'i, who lived under Umayyad rule, no doubt tried to validate a practice which several Umayyad Caliphs were forced to adopt in their treaty relations with the Byzantines."[68]

The obligation of Jihad can and should be suspended under only one circumstance: the probability of military defeat. Non-Islamic states (with the possible exception of Ethiopia) can expect nothing more than a truce with Islam. This truce is not based upon both sides' unwillingness to engage in battle, but on Islam's calculation of its relative weakness.

---

[67] Khadduri, *War and Peace in the Law of Islam*, 134.
[68] Khadduri, *War and Peace in the Law of Islam*, 134-136.

It follows that in Muslim legal theory, defeat is an anomaly which could be tolerated only under *force majeur*; thus the imam is advised either to abstain from going to war if his forces are insufficient to attain victory, or, if he should suffer defeat, to withdraw and save the lives of surviving believers. Defeated Muslims always maintained that their battle with the enemy would be resumed, however long they had to wait for the second round.[69]

Illustrative of this concept is the response by the Malaysian Prime Minister to the 11 February 2003 audio tape, purportedly from Usama bin Laden, in which he calls for Muslim war over U.S. threats against Iraq. Prime Minister Mahathir Mohamad answered: "It's a stupid idea. We want to fight a holy war if we can win. If we go in just to be killed, that's not [holy war]."[70]

The opposite is also true. If you can win a Jihad, there is an obligation to fight. *"So be not weak and ask not for peace* (from the enemies of Islam) *while you are having the upper hand"* [47:35]. This verse instructs Muslims not to be weak in confronting the enemy and seek peace, an end of war and cessation of hostilities with unbelievers, if Muslims have the upper hand in strength, men and equipment; seeking peace in this state is a sign of cowardice.[71]

The dar al-Islam is in perpetual war with the dar al-Harb. Other conditions of relationships between Islam and the rest of the world are forced upon Islam through weakness. Failing this weakness in Islam, the world would have been transformed into the dar al-Islam, and, in theory, be at peace. Within dar al-Islam, by definition, shari'a would prevail and regulate the peaceful relationship among the peoples (all being either Muslims or dhimmis) of the world.

> The Jihad...was regarded as Islam's instrument to transform the dar al-Harb into dar al-Islam. If that end had ever been achieved, the dar al-Harb would have been reduced to non-existence and the raison d'etre of the Jihad, except perhaps for combating Islam's internal enemies, would eventually have disappeared. We may argue, therefore, that in Islamic legal theory, the ultimate objective of Islam was not war per se, but the ultimate establishment of peace. This may be regarded as another reason why the Jihad was not made...the sixth pillar of faith, since in theory it was merely a temporary instrument to establish ultimate peace, rather than a permanent article of the faith.[72]

The Jihad, accordingly, may be stated as a doctrine of a permanent state of war, not a continuous fighting. Thus some jurists argued that the mere preparation for the Jihad is a fulfillment of its obligations. The state, however, must

---

[69] Khadduri, *War and Peace in the Law of Islam*, 136.

[70] "Arabs Ignore Bin Laden War Call," *Washington Times*, online ed., 13 February 2003, URL: <http://www.washingtontimes.com>, accessed 13 February 2003.

[71] Abualrub, *Holy War Crusades Jihad: In the Torah, the Gospels, and the Quran*, 172.

[72] Khadduri, *War and Peace in the Law of Islam*, 141.

be prepared militarily not only to repel a sudden attack on Islam, but also to use its forces for offensive purposes when the Caliph deems it necessary to do so."[73]

The duality of Islam — shari'a as a theoretical vehicle for peaceful relations among Muslims and dhimmis, and war with the rest of the world — is rooted in the two periods of Mohammad's career. "The Meccan chapters of the Qur'an deal chiefly with the unity of God, the wickedness of idolatry, and the imminence of divine judgment. Their stated purpose is to bring an Arabic revelation to the Arabs such as had previously been vouchsafed to other peoples in their own languages."[74]

> It is clear that the saying "more slayeth word than sword" cannot be applied to his work in the Medinese period. Emigration from Mecca put an end to the time when he was to "turn away from the idolaters" (15:94) or merely summon them "to the way of God through wisdom and good admonition" (16:125). It was now time for a different watchword: "When the sacred months are over, kill the idolaters wherever you find them; take them prisoner, lay siege to them, and wait for them in every ambush" (9:5); "fight in the way of God" (2:244).....He [Mohammed] brought the sword into the world; he did not merely "smite the earth with the rod of his mouth, and with the breath of his lips slay the wicked." The trumpet he sounded was real enough. Real blood clung to the sword he wielded to establish his realm.[75]

Thus, within the Qur'an can be found both the peaceful preachings of the Prophet, and the motivation to conduct Jihad. Islam is a peaceful religion that is in perpetual (but not necessarily constant) warfare with the dar al-Harb. "This obligation [Jihad] is without limit of time or space. It must continue until the whole world has either accepted the Islamic faith or submitted to the power of the Islamic state."[76]

As already mentioned, it was obvious by the 10th century A.D. that the "lightning" global victory of Islam would not occur. The realization that relations with external powers must somehow be regulated within shari'a also impacted the conduct of the Jihad.

> When Muslim power began to decline, Muslim publicists seem to have tacitly admitted that in principle the Jihad as a permanent state of war had become obsolete; it was no longer compatible with Muslim interests. The concept of the Jihad as a state of war underwent certain changes. This change, as a matter of fact, did not imply abandonment of Jihad duty, it only meant the entry of the obligation into a period of suspension — it assumed a dormant status, from which the imam may revive it at any time he deems

---

[73] Khadduri, *War and Peace in the Law of Islam*, 64.
[74] Lewis, *The Arabs in History*, 35-36.
[75] Goldziher, *Introduction to Islamic Theology and Law*, 23.
[76] Lewis, *The Political Language of Islam*, 73.

necessary. In practice, however, the Muslims came to think of this as more of a normal condition than an active Jihad.[77]

Even in this period of retreat, the offensive Jihad was by no means abandoned. As late as 1896, the Afghans invaded the mountainous region of the Hindu Kush in what is now northeastern Afghanistan. Until then the inhabitants were not Muslim.... During the same period Jihads of various kinds were conducted in Africa against non-Muslim populations. But for the most part, the concept, practice, and experience of Jihad in the modern Islamic world have been overwhelmingly defensive.[78]

Jihad, because it is a religious obligation, is governed by a complex set of shari'a (religious law). Aside from the correctness of declaring or fighting in a Jihad, the conduct of the Jihad is regulated. Bin Laden's apparent conduct of his Jihad against the United States also leaves him open for criticism. For example, instances of Al-Qa'ida members swearing bay'a to him may be questioned by even dedicated, non-Al-Qa'ida jihadists. Bay'a is the pledge of homage or allegiance to the Caliph.[79]

While the ceremonies and rituals of investiture vary from time to time and from place to place, one part was universal, and was seen by jurists and theologians on the one hand, and political and military leaders on the other, as the essential act of validation, by which the sovereign accepted the duties of a Muslim head of state and received the power to discharge them, and the subjects undertook the duty of obedience to him. This act, in Arabic [is] called the bay'a....Under the Caliphs, though the ceremonies became more complex and more elaborate, the bay'a remained the central symbol of the investiture of sovereignty."[80]

Another part of the bay'a was the Caliph's/Sultan's commitment to uphold the shari'a and to rely on the ulema for legitimacy, at the same time using them as instruments of influence.[81]

Even some jihadists have problems with some of the methods used by Al-Qa'ida. There is no debate about the attacks on the *USS Cole* and the Pentagon, both of which could be considered legitimate (assuming that a proper Jihad existed). The attacks on U.S. Embassies (in which hundreds of Africans, many of whom are Muslim, and few Americans are killed), and the attack on the World Trade Center (also killing innocent civilians and Muslims), are, however, problematic.

---

[77] Khadduri, *War and Peace in the Law of Islam*, 65.
[78] Lewis, *The Crisis of Islam*, 36.
[79] Khadduri, *War and Peace in the Law of Islam*, 297.
[80] Lewis, *The Political Language of Islam*, 58.
[81] Interview with Dr. Max Gross, Dean, School of Intelligence Studies, Joint Military Intelligence College, 27 August 2003.

The use of nuclear, biological and chemical weapons is also a subject of shari'a controversy. In these cases, however, Al-Qa'ida may be on firm shari'a ground. There were instances such as when in A.D. 632 the Caliph Abu Bakr enjoined his army not to practice treachery or mutilation, or to kill a child, an old man, or a woman, or a monk.[82] "The Maliki jurist Khalil advises against the use of poisoned arrows and Hilli goes so far as to prohibit their use in any form against the enemy."[83] "The Prophet Muhammed was against the practice of treacherous killing and mutilation, but when the Makkans did not respect this rule he ordered his followers to retaliate."[84] Jihad is a bloody business, and was conducted as such. The accepted rules included not only the use of poisons, but the killing, when necessary, of Muslims. "The jihadists are permitted to besiege cities....Poison, blood, or any material that may spoil the drinking water may be thrown into the water supplies or canals to force the enemy to capitulate. Poisoned arrows, and arrows carrying bundles of fire, are ordinarily permitted to be used."[85]

> Sufyan al-Thawri and Abu Hanifa permitted attack even if shooting by arrows or hurling machines would kill the believers; provided that the jihadists intend to shoot the unbelievers; the killing of believers (including women and children) would be regarded as killing by mistake. Shafi'i advises attack on the fortified places and castles, but not on the houses; if however, fighting was at close range, they ought not abstain from shooting, even if it results in killing believers. Ghazzali, a Shafi'i jurist-theologian, justifies the shooting of believers in attacking the harbis [one who belongs to dar al-Harb] on the ground of *istislah*, or public interest; that is, the killing of a few believers is justified on the grounds that it would serve the greater interests of the Muslim community.[86]

Al-Qa'ida has made its reputation, as did Lebanese Hizballah, Palestinian Hamas, Fatah's Al Aqsa Martyrs Brigades, and Islamic Jihad, on martyrdom operations that were pre-planned as "suicides." This method of Jihad is highly dubious. The group in Islam that is famous for apparent "suicide" operations is the Shi'a Ismaili sect known as the "Assassins." This sect sent members to kill dignitaries in close quarters by use of a dagger. It was not expected that the assassin would return. The Ismaili's, however, were careful to not in fact commit suicide. "The Assassin himself, having struck down his assigned victim, made no attempt to escape, nor was any attempt made to rescue him. On the contrary, to have survived a mission was seen as a disgrace."[87] It was left to the victims followers to deal with the "assassin." "Committing suicide is one of the major sins that, according to some Muslim scholars, annuls one's Islamic faith. It was the Prophet's practice not to lead the Funeral Prayer for those who committed suicide."[88] "Jihad or otherwise, suicide and

---

[82] Lewis, *The Political Language of Islam*, 75.

[83] Khadduri, *War and Peace in the Law of Islam*, 104.

[84] Khadduri, *War and Peace in the Law of Islam,* 106

[85] Khadduri, *War and Peace in the Law of Islam,* 106.

[86] Khadduri, *War and Peace in the Law of Islam*, 107.

[87] Lewis, *The Assassins: A Radical Sect in Islam*, XII.

[88] Abualrub, *Holy War Crusades Jihad: In the Torah, the Gospels, and the Quran*, 209.

suicide missions are strictly prohibited in Islam. The Shaikhs or groups who condone, encourage and permit suicide missions and call them Jihad, are transgressing the limits of Allah and leading their followers to certain demise."[89]

> In this respect [making no attempt to escape], and only in this respect, the Assassins may indeed be regarded as the forerunners of the suicide bombers of today. But in an important respect the suicide bomber marks a radical departure from earlier belief and practice. Islam has always strongly condemned suicide, regarding it as a major sin. The suicide forfeits any claim he may have to paradise, however strong, and is doomed to eternal punishment in hell, where his torment will consist of the unending repetition of the act by which he committed suicide. A clear difference was made between throwing oneself to certain death at the hands of an overwhelmingly strong enemy, and dying by one's own hand. The first, if conducted in a properly authorized holy war, was a passport to heaven; the second to damnation. The blurring of this previously vital distinction was the work of some twentieth-century theologians who outlined the new theory which the suicide bombers put into practice.[90]

Reinforcing this "new theory" of suicide bombers is the reverence paid to the successful suicide bomber in his community (this is especially true in the Palestinian territories), and the payments made by Muslim governments and charities to the suicide's family. The community and family celebrate the "martyrdom," not the "damnation."

Attacking U.S. personnel and facilities in non-Muslim nations may be permissible, assuming that the Jihad is valid, but there is a problem with attacking those personnel and facilities in Muslim nations. Islam, although reluctant for Muslims to live "abroad" in the dar al-Harb, recognized the practical benefits of allowing non-Muslims to "visit" dar al-Islam. "The visitor or temporary resident from abroad was called musta'min, the holder of an aman, or safe conduct....The musta'min was exempt from the poll tax and many of the other disabilities imposed on the dhimmi, but enjoyed the same right of living by his own laws and under his own chief, in this case usually the consul of his city or country. The aman was granted for a limited time and could be renewed. If the musta'min overstayed his aman he became a dhimmi."[91] "The Muslim is under obligation to abstain from doing any harm or injury to non-Muslims as long as he enjoys the benefits of their amans."[92] If one recognizes the legitimacy of a Muslim government, which of course Al-Qa'ida and other jihadists don't normally do, then an attack on foreigners who are in that country with permission of that Muslim government would be prohibited.

---

[89] Abualrub, *Holy War Crusades Jihad: In the Torah, the Gospels, and the Quran*, 211.

[90] Lewis, *The Assassins: A Radical Sect in Islam*, XII.

[91] Lewis, *Islam and the West*, 48.

[92] Khadduri, *War and Peace in the Law of Islam*, 172.

WEAKNESS BREEDS JIHAD

Why has Jihad, which had been generally "suspended" following World War One, been revived in a new and more virulent form? What is different about, and fuels "modern Jihad"? As long as Islam was strong militarily, it endeavored to expand, albeit with accommodations to temporary imbalances in forces. This was at first an Arab expansion and then a Turkish one. The Turkish defeat in Vienna in 1683 set the Ottoman Empire on a downward spiral that continually highlighted its military inferiority to the Western nations. By its final collapse in World War One, the lone Islamic world power could not rally Muslims to Jihad. Arabs had in fact fought on the side of the British against the Turks. "The end of this phase came with the abortive Ottoman Jihad proclaimed in 1914 against the Allied and Associated powers. This Jihad — contemptuously styled 'the holy war made in Germany' by the Dutch Islamicist Snouck Hurgronje — failed utterly in its purpose of arousing the Muslim soldiers in the British, French and Russian imperial armies against their European masters"[93] This was at a time when the last Caliph still resided in Istanbul, and was legally able to call the faithful to Jihad. With the fall of the Ottoman Empire, the last Muslim world power disappeared. There has been no Muslim power that has arisen to take its place. Today, despite, or more likely because of this fact, there is no Muslim world power, Jihad has re-emerged, and of necessity has assumed a different form.

Shari'a is clear on two points of Jihad that must be overcome for modern jihadists to gain legitimacy. Jihad is the purview of the Muslim ruler, and it should not be conducted from a position of Muslim weakness. To accomplish this, Al-Qa'ida jihadists alter the concept of defensive Jihad. Instead of dealing with a sudden enemy attack upon the Muslims, these jihadists see a general attack against all of Islam (or more properly the concepts of Islam as a religion). What to Western analysis would seem as a growing, not narrowing, gap between the relative strength of dar al-Islam and dar al-Harb, is viewed by the modern Al-Qa'ida jihadist as shifting in Islam's favor. In measuring relative strength, the jihadist puts great weight on the willingness of the individual to be martyred. Thus, if the world's 1.2 billion Muslims could be brought to Jihad (obviously not all, but a large number) Allah will reward them with victory. Instead of the traditional two-to-one strength ratio cited in the Qur'an (because Allah "knows that there is a weakness amongst you"), jihadists look to an early Muslim victory over the Persians. "Tabari reports that the Muslim force at the battle of al-Qadisiyya (A.D. 637) was made up of 12,000 men against 120,000 Persians."[94] This battle demonstrates that everything is possible with Allah. This view was further reinforced by what Al-Qa'ida viewed as a weakness in the West, and especially the United States. By the very conduct of Jihad, Islamists hope to force the correlation of forces to favor Jihad. Al-Qa'ida operations are not only designed to weaken the economic and psychological fabric of America, but, more importantly, in doing so to bring Muslims to Jihad.

---

[93] Lewis, *The Political Language of Islam*, 146.
[94] Khadduri, *War and Peace in the Law of Islam*, 89.

Why did Al-Qa'ida declare Jihad against the United States in 1996? The simple answer is a combination of the American threat coupled with a perception of American weakness. Usama bin Laden and Ayatollah Khomeini share a similar view of the threat posed by the United States.

> For Usama bin Ladin, his declaration of war against the United States marks the resumption of the struggle for religious dominance of the world that began in the seventh century. For him and his followers, this is a moment of opportunity. Today, America exemplifies the civilization and embodies the leadership of the House of War, and like Rome and Byzantium, it has become degenerate and demoralized, ready to be overthrown. But despite its weakness, it is also dangerous. Khomeini's designation of the United States as "the Great Satan" was telling, and for the members of Al-Qa'ida it is the seduction of America and its profligate, dissolute way of life that represents the greatest kind of threat to the kind of Islam they wish to impose on their fellow Muslims.[95]

Indicative of this "fundamentalist" view of a threat to Islam from any source that represents modernization was the reaction in the Hijaz area of Arabia to a perception that the Ottoman's were taking their modernization efforts too far.

> The first example comes from the holy city of Mecca, then part of the Ottoman Empire, in April 1855. In that year, reports, only partially accurate, were reaching the holy cities of certain reforms on which the Ottoman government was alleged to be embarking, including such major departures from existing practice as the abolition of black slavery, the granting of equal rights to Christians, and the emancipation of women. The chief of the ulema of Mecca, a certain Sheikh Jamal, issued a fatwa, or "ruling," denouncing all these projected and rumored innovations: "The ban on slaves is contrary to shari'a. Furthermore...permitting women to walk unveiled, giving women the right to initiate divorce, and such like are contrary to pure divine law.... With such proposals the Turks have become infidels. Their blood is forfeit, and it is lawful to make their children slaves." The fatwa was followed by a proclamation of Jihad against the Ottomans, and a revolt against their authority.[96]

Non-Muslims are still not allowed in Mecca, nor welcomed as permanent residents in Saudi Arabia. Women's freedoms are curtailed in most of the Muslim world. Slavery was not abolished in Yemen and Saudi Arabia until 1962.[97] Black slavery is still practiced in the southern Sudan.

Contrary to a Western-centric view of the world, where opposition to European powers has been viewed as a political reaction to European ideologies, a motivation for opposing

---

[95] Lewis, *The Crisis of Islam,* 162-163.
[96] Lewis, *The Political Language of Islam,* 89.
[97] Lewis, *What Went Wrong,* 89.

Western values in the Islamic world has consistently been associated with the perceived negative impact of Western values on Islam. The prospect of Jihad was constantly "bubbling up," but was ruthlessly suppressed, and thus contained. Recent Islamic victories, however, have spread Jihad over always-fertile ground.

> Some Muslims opposed foreign domination and domestic change in the name not of their nation or country or class but of their faith, and saw the real danger as the loss of Islamic values and the real enemy, at home even more than abroad, as those who sought to replace Islamic laws and obligations by others derived from secular or, as they would put it, infidel sources. There have been several such movements of Islamic defense and renewal: the Wahhabi rising against the Ottomans at the turn of the eighteenth and nineteenth centuries; the resistance of the religious devotees of Ahmad Brelwi to the British in northern India (1826-1831); of Shamil to the Russians in Daghestan (1830-1859); of 'Abd al-Qadir to the French in Algeria (1832-1847); the pan-Islamic movement against the European powers in the late nineteenth and early twentieth centuries; the resistance of the Basmachis and other Islamic rebels against Soviet power in the 1920's; the brief upsurge of radical Islamic movements in the Arab lands and Iran in the late 1940s and early 1950s. All of these were crushed and their leaders killed or rendered innocuous. The first to achieve success and to gain and retain power was the Islamic revolution which began in Iran in 1979. The impact of that success was felt all over the Islamic world.[98]

The fall of the Shah of Iran, America's premier Muslim ally in the Middle East, was viewed differently by Americans and Islamists. To the Carter administration the fall of the Shah represented an internal Iranian issue. In fact, given the so-called reformers that surrounded the Ayatollah Khomeini, it could have been seen as a "benign" event, leading to a liberal government that Washington could deal with. It took years for America to realize that their ally was overthrown by an Islamic revolution, inimical to U.S. interests. In a time when the Middle East was viewed in terms of nations and resources, the importance of Islam was ignored. To the Islamist, the ease with which the Shah fell, without U.S. attempts at intervention, showed U.S. weakness, especially since U.S. intervention restored him to the throne in 1953, and because of the shabby treatment by the U.S. afterward, not allowing him asylum until he was almost dead, and even then "allowing" him to leave U.S. medical care under Islamist pressure.

> Different groups in the region drew two lessons from these events — one, that the Americans were willing to use both force and intrigue to install or restore their puppet rulers in Middle Eastern countries; the other, that they were not reliable patrons when these puppets were seriously attacked by their own people; and would simply abandon them. The one evoked hatred, the other contempt — a dangerous combination.[99]

---

[98] Lewis, *Islam and the West*, 39.
[99] Lewis, *The Crisis of Islam*, 76.

Pre-dating the Islamic revolution in Iran, but coincident with it from an historical perspective, was the October 1973 Arab-Israeli war. This war, although a battlefield defeat for the Egyptian and Syrian armies that attacked Israel, became a strategic, and more importantly, a psychological Arab victory. The fact that it was the United States that forced Israel to spare the Egyptian third army and not march on Cairo, and forced an Israeli withdrawal from the gates of Damascus, is long forgotten. For the Arabs, this war represented a victory, still celebrated, over Israel and the West.

> After humiliation and frustration came a third component, necessary for the resurgence [of revolutionary Islam] — a new confidence and sense of power. These arose from the oil crisis of 1973, when in support of Egypt's war against Israel, the oil-producing Arab countries used both the supply and the price of oil as what proved to be a very effective weapon. The resulting wealth, pride, and self-assurance were reinforced by another new element — contempt. On closer acquaintance with Europe and America, Muslim visitors began to observe and describe what they saw as the moral degeneracy and consequent weakness of Western civilization."[100]

The "Great Satan" is thus an existential threat to Islam, but also is perceived as weak and ready to be defeated. It is this combination of threat and weakness that requires the Jihad against the United States. The exact start of the chain of events that led Al-Qa'ida to believe in the weakness of the dar al-Harb and the United States in particular, is difficult to determine. What is certain is that by his declaration of Jihad in 1996, bin Laden believed in U.S. weakness. This was to remain the case until after 11 September 2001, when the U.S. readily defeated the Taliban government in Afghanistan and scattered Al-Qa'ida and other jihadists. The U.S. military victory in Iraq in April 2003 only reinforces the view among many jihadists that Al-Qa'ida made a fundamental error in attacking the United States. Hard-core jihadists, however, view the war in Afghanistan as only beginning, similar to what the Soviets faced after their initial victories in 1979, the U.S. will now face a protracted guerrilla war, and ultimate defeat. Vietnam is viewed as a parallel for both Afghanistan, and now Iraq, where the U.S. will not demonstrate staying power.

The string of U.S. defeats vis-à-vis Islam only begins with the overthrow of the Shah of Iran in 1979. The U.S. failure to support its longtime regional friend and ally was viewed as a pattern that made all Muslim governments vulnerable. The subsequent Tehran "hostage crisis" and U.S. failure to take effective action (witness the debacle of Operation DESERT ONE) against Iran reinforced the perception of U.S. weakness and lack of will. Preceding this was one of several "defeats" of U.S. ally Israel. As noted, the October 1973 Arab-Israeli war, by most measures a defeat for Arab armies, is viewed by the Arabs as a victory. President Anwar Sadat of Egypt was killed by jihadists, for example, during an October War "victory" parade in 1981. Ironically, the Arabs fail to take into consideration that it was U.S. restraints on Israel that prevented a more complete Arab defeat and promoted subsequent negotiations that allowed Egypt and Syria to gain land that they had

---

[100]Lewis, *The Crisis of Islam*, 22.

lost both in 1967 and 1973. The October War, and resulting Arab oil embargo, also demonstrated a potential Arab economic weapon to be used against the U.S. Further, the Israeli invasion of Lebanon in 1982, and their subsequent forced withdrawal from Beirut and a U.S. Marine presence (ironically in large part to save Yasser Arafat and the PLO), led to three U.S. defeats. The U.S. Embassy was bombed twice (1983 and 1984), but more telling, the U.S. Marine Barracks in Beirut was bombed in 1983 with the loss of over 200 lives. The U.S. reaction was a withdrawal of forces from Lebanon. This occurred while the jihadists were fighting a determined Soviet Union in Afghanistan. The Afghan jihadists, from whence Al-Qa'ida originates, could not help but contrast Islam's easy victory over the U.S. and its Israeli ally in Lebanon with their hard-fought victory over the Soviet Union in Afghanistan. If they could defeat the "superior" Soviet threat, why should they not attack the U.S.? In fact, if Allah chose to give them victory over the mighty Soviet Union, what right did they have not to engage the U.S.?

U.S. weakness (like it or not, in the jihadist mind there is no difference between the U.S. and Israel, and U.S. failure to support Israel is viewed as U.S. weakness) continued to be demonstrated for the next two decades. The Israeli Embassy (1992) and a Jewish cultural center/school (1994) were blown up in Buenos Aires without retribution. The 1996 Khobar Towers attack against the U.S. in Saudi Arabia again went without retribution. The U.S. response to the attempted assassination, in 1993, of former President George Bush, was also viewed as weak. The Palestinians launched an *Intifada* that Israel was constrained by the U.S. and Europe from putting down. This Intifada electrified the Muslim world. It also demonstrated that when faced with force, the U.S. was willing to negotiate rather than fight. The entire effort by the Clinton administration to broker a Palestinian-Israeli "peace" agreement did nothing to enhance the U.S. stature among jihadists (or for anyone else in the Middle East, for that matter). The 1993 Oslo Accords, hailed as a major move toward Palestinian-Israeli peace, and since discredited, opened the Palestinian areas to the advent of suicide bombers from Hamas, Islamic Jihad and elements of *Fatah*. The personal involvement of the U.S. President, and the subsequent rebuff by Yasser Arafat, validated years of a perception of U.S. weakness. The image of Madeleine Albright, U.S. Secretary of State, chasing Yasser Arafat down the hall of a French palace to implore him to return to negotiations must have been particularly indicative of U.S. weakness.

Until recently, bin Laden ignored the Palestinians. In fact, a U.S. abandonment of Israel, while likely garnering "good press" in the Arab world, would be perceived as weakness. An Israeli defeat at the hands of the Palestinian jihadists, to include a withdrawal from the West Bank, would be a major victory, and coupled with their perceived victory over the Soviet Union, would further embolden jihadists to attack the U.S. While the U.S. may want to force Israel to allow the creation of a Palestinian state on surrendered West Bank land, and establish Middle East "peace" for other reasons, this action would not benefit the counter-Jihad.

Indicative of the U.S. lack of realization of the impact of its actions in showing weakness to jihadists was the operation in Somalia in 1993. For the U.S. this was a humanitarian mission that went wrong. For the jihadists (and many Arabs) this was yet another stinging defeat for the U.S. by poorly armed but motivated Muslims. This is also a prime example of the U.S.'s not realizing that it was in a Jihad. Somalia resulted in an anti-U.S., jihadist presence in east Africa which led to the 1998 bombings of the U.S. embassies in Kenya and Tanzania. The U.S. response to this action was rather tepid, as was the response to the October 2000 attack on the *USS Cole* in Aden. Coincident with the U.S. operation in Somalia was the first attack on the World Trade Center in 1993. An attack on U.S. soil by jihadists was treated as a terrorist/criminal act. Again, the U.S. did not realize that it was in a Jihad. The final indicator of U.S. weakness was the Israeli withdrawal, under U.S. pressure, from Lebanon in May 2000. The Clinton Administration was instrumental in aiding the election of Ehud Barak as Israeli Prime Minister. Barak literally withdrew Israeli forces from Lebanon, overnight, and in a sense "under fire." The message was clear; Lebanese Hizballah had won victories over the U.S. and Israel by applying force. The two great antagonists in the dar al-Harb, Israel and the U.S., had no staying power.

What was Usama bin Laden's "view from the mountain" when he decided to declare Jihad and attack the United States? He had just participated in a successful Jihad against the Soviet Union that forced that great power's withdrawal from Afghanistan (1989). A Taliban government, representing a Central Asian "Caliphate" had been established in Afghanistan. Jihadists from Afghanistan had participated in a nearly successful war in Tajikistan (1992-1997) which has left Islamists (former United Tajik Opposition) officials in key government positions. Again, the U.S. did not treat the "Tajik Civil War" as a skirmish in Jihad. Although it was clear that one side had strong Islamist credentials, overall, the war was considered to be a regional dispute within Tajikistan. Successful operations, from Afghanistan and Tajikistan, were being launched by the Uzbek Islamic Movement (UIM) against Uzbekistan. Other jihadist attacks were occurring against Kyrgyzstan. An Islamic government had taken hold in Sudan. Jihadists were "successfully" challenging the secular government in Algeria. The Russians were defeated in the first Chechen war (1994-96). Islam was on the rise, and the dar al-Harb was weak. Jihad was called for, but the Muslim governments refused to engage. The 1991 Gulf War, as opposed to showing U.S. strength, as did Operation Iraqi Freedom in 2003, showed a lack of U.S. resolve to finish the job. It did, however, leave the intolerable presence of U.S. forces in Saudi Arabia and the Gulf. This presence, directed against the Muslim state of Iraq, and supported by the Muslim state of Saudi Arabia, Kuwait and all other Gulf states, showed to bin Laden the unnecessary weakness of Arab rulers in the face of the U.S.

> Bin Ladin's remarks in an interview with John Miller, of ABC News, on May 28, 1998, are especially revealing: "We have seen in the last decade the decline of the American government and the weakness of the American soldier, who is ready to wage cold wars and unprepared to fight long wars. This was proven in Beirut when the Marines fled after two explosions. It also proves they can run in less than twenty-four hours, and this was also repeated in Somalia...[Our] youth were surprised at the low morale of the American soldiers....After a few blows they ran in defeat....They forgot about being the

world leader and the leader of the new world order. [They] left, dragging their corpses and their shameful defeat."[101]

For Usama bin Laden, and all jihadists, the Jihad has the ultimate aim of establishing the dar al-Islam. The belief by the U.S. that a Jihad could be unleashed against the Soviet Union in Afghanistan, and then ended when the Soviets were defeated, showed a basic lack of understanding of Islam. Many jihadists left Afghanistan and returned to their home countries to continue their Jihad against their own Muslim governments that refused to institute, or sufficiently institute, shari'a. Others became "professional jihadists" fighting in Afghanistan, Tajikistan, Chechnya, Bosnia, and elsewhere. Still others, to include bin Laden, and eventually Al-Qa'ida, chose to conduct Jihad against the only remaining major power in dar al-Harb, the U.S. From his perspective, he could do nothing else. Islam was on the rise, the Soviet Union/Russia was defeated, and the U.S. was weak. Any reason for the suspension of a global Jihad had ended. The fall of the twin towers on 9/11 reinforced this view. Allah provided the victory of the towers' complete collapse. The result of the U.S. response (especially the rapid ending of the Afghan Caliphate), however, has led to doubt throughout the jihadist ranks, as to the degree of Allah's support for this Jihad.

---

[101]Lewis, The Crisis of Islam, 162.

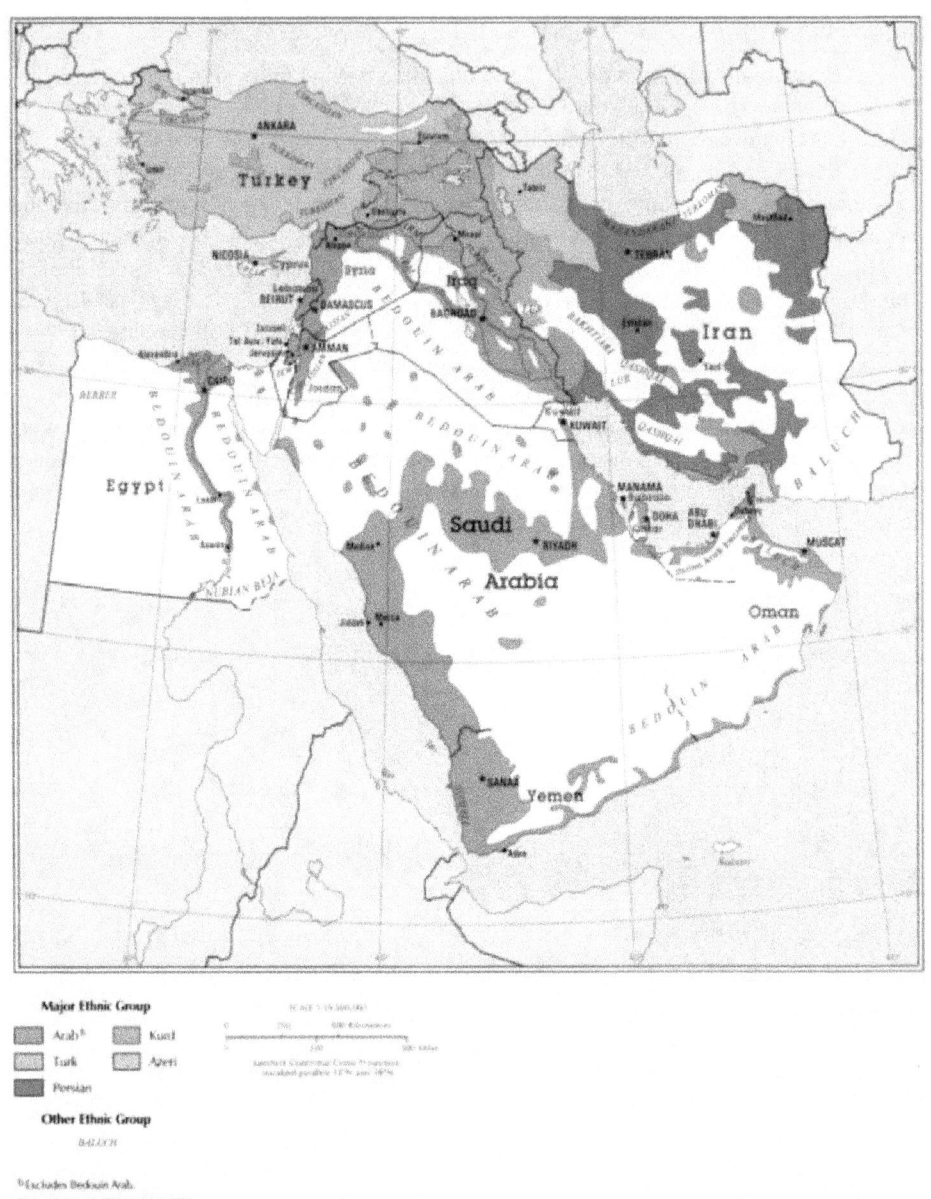

Figure 3. (U) Source: CIA, Atlas of the Middle East, 1993, 15. (Data from 1993).

MODERN JIHAD: HATE WRAPPED IN RELIGION

It is clear that jihadists in general, and Al-Qa'ida, in particular, are not practicing classical Islam. They have, however, achieved almost universal support for their goals in the Muslim community, because their ultimate message is an Islamic one, fight for dar al-Islam. It is a message that is impossible for a Muslim not to support. What drives Al-Qa'ida, and some other jihadists, is a hatred for the United States, Christianity, and especially Judaism.

> But...there was and unfortunately still is a profound, pervasive, and passionate hatred of the West and all that it represents, as a world power, as an ideology, as a way of life, and that hatred is extended to embrace a wide range of local Westernizers and modernizers. It is a hatred so deep that it has led those who feel it to rally to any plausible enemy of the West — even a racist like Hitler who despised Arabs, an atheist like Stalin who suppressed Islam, a gangster like Saddam Hussein who violated every rule of Arab decency and Islamic morality.[102]

> It is easy to understand the rage of the traditional Muslim confronted with the modern world. Schooled in a religious culture in which, from the very beginning, rightness has meant supremacy, he has seen that supremacy lost in the world to Western power; lost in his own country to foreign intruders, with their foreign ways and their Westernized protégés; lost in his home to emancipated women and rebellious children.[103]

An interesting and recent Sunni manifestation of contempt and disgust of Westerners is a reversion to a classic practice of not coming into physical contact with a "non-believer." Over time Sunnis, had relaxed this standard that is now making a comeback.

> On examining the legal documents, we find that the Shi'a legal position toward other faiths is much harsher and stiffer than that taken by Sunni Muslims. Their law reveals a heightened intolerance to people of other beliefs. The Shi'a interpretation of the law had no use for the orthodox Sunni mitigation of certain narrow-minded old conceptions. Of the severe rule in the Qur'an (9:28) that "unbelievers are unclean," Sunni Islam has accepted an interpretation that is as good as a repeal. Shi'a law, on the other hand, has maintained the literal sense of the rule; it declares the bodily substance of the unbeliever to be ritually unclean, and lists the touching of the unbeliever among the ten things that produce *najasa*, ritual impurity.[104]

---

[102]Lewis, *Islam in History*, 410.

[103]Lewis, *Islam and the West*, 39.

[104]Goldziher, *Introduction to Islamic Theology and Law,* 213.

The Islamist message is that "Islam is the Answer." It is the answer to their poverty, backwardness, and especially their weakness vis-à-vis the West. It is the Christians and Jews, represented by colonialist Europe and the "Great Satan" America that have victimized the Muslim (read Arab) world. It is false Muslim leaders that have embraced Western concepts of nationalism, secularism, and socialism that have resulted in the subjugation of Islam. Allowing the cultural dominance of Islam by the U.S. is worse, and presents a greater threat to Islam, than did the earlier political and economic dominance of Europe. In fact, a colonialist U.S. could be more readily accepted than a culturally aggressive U.S. Going back to the early precepts of Islam, before all of this corruption, is therefore the answer to this culturally based challenge. What the jihadists and Islamists (not all Islamists take up arms in Jihad) fail to recognize, and would never admit, is that if Islam does not embody the answer, then it may be the problem.

> Until very recently, history — that is to say significant, usable history — for Muslim historians meant the history of Islam. And of the events in the history of Islam, the most significant, thus the most usable, were those of the early centuries, the life of the Prophet and his immediate successors, which constitute the sacred history, one might even say the salvation history, of Islam and form the core of the historical self-awareness of Muslims everywhere.[105]

It is from this period — the time of the Qu'ran, and of the documented sayings of the Prophet (hadiths) — that Muslim jurisprudence is drawn. Theologians agonize over this period to determine the proper course for the addressable future, based upon the actions of the Prophets and his companions. Jihadists take a selective view of this period, emphasizing the glorious expansion of Islam through battle. They also take a selective view of Islamic history that ignores internal strife, dissension, and murder among the companions and their families following Muhammed's death. They ignore the long history of Umayyad, Abbasid, Turk, and Persian rulers of Islam that were more "corrupt" than current Muslim rulers. In short, modern Islamists and jihadists want to return to a time in Islamic history that was largely a fiction.

The Islamic jurists who support the modern Jihad cannot be unaware of Islam's history that shows anything but a single, united dar al-Islam fighting the dar al-Harb. They must choose to ignore history in order to facilitate the indoctrination of their followers. In fact, Muslim-on-Muslim violence occurred immediately following the Prophet's death.

> The death of Muhammad [on 8 June 632] confronted the infant Muslim community with something in the nature of a constitutional crisis. The Prophet had left no provision for the succession, nor had he even created a council on the lines of the tribal Majlis [council of elders] which might have exercised authority during the crucial transition period....The concept of legitimate succession was foreign to the Arabs at the time, and it is probable that even if Muhammad had left a son the sequence of events would not

---

[105]Lewis, *The Political Language of Islam*, 9.

have been different....The Arabs had only one precedent to guide them — the election of a new tribal chief. The Medinese proceeded to choose one from among the tribe of Kazraj, thus incidentally revealing the limitations of their conversion.... The crisis was met by three men: Abu Bakr, 'Umar, and Abu 'Ubayda, who by swift and resolute action installed Abu Bakr as ruler in place of the Prophet.[106] "The first task of the new regime was to counter by military action a movement among the tribes known to tradition as the *Ridda*....The refusal of the tribes or [sic] recognize the succession of Abu Bakr was in effect not so much a relapse by converted Muslims to their previous paganism, but rather the simple and automatic termination of a political contract by the death of one of the parties. The tribes nearest to Medina had no doubt been converted and their interests were so closely identified with those of the Umma [all Muslims as a people] that their separate history has not been recorded. For the rest, the death of Muhammad automatically severed their bonds with Medina, and the parties, in accordance with ancient custom, resumed their liberty of action. To restore the hegemony of Medina, Abu Bakr had to make new treaties. While some of the nearer tribes accepted these, the more distant ones refused, and Abu Bakr was compelled to undertake the military subjugation of these tribes as a prelude to their conversion.[107]

Abu Bakr served as Caliph (successor to the Prophet Muhammad, and chief of state) for only two years. 'Umar succeeded him without apparent strife. "On 4 November 644 the Caliph 'Umar was murdered by a Persian slave."[108] He was followed by 'Uthman ibn 'Affan, a Meccan, a member of the family of Umayya, and the sole representative of the leading Meccan patricians among the early companions of the Prophet with sufficient prestige to rank as a candidate.[109] Opposition to 'Uthman was centered in Medina, led by Talha and Zubayr, two disgruntled Meccans, and by 'Amr, who was replaced as an official in Egypt, and A'isha, the widow of the Prophet.[110]

On 17 June 656 a party of mutineers from the Arab army in Egypt, who had come to Medina to present their grievances, entered the Caliph's quarters and wounded him mortally. The murder marks a turning point in the history of Islam. The slaying of a Caliph by rebellious Muslims established an ominous precedent and gravely weakened the religious and moral prestige of the office as a bond of unity in Islam.... 'Ali [the cousin and son-in-law of the Prophet] was almost immediately hailed as successor in Medina, but even some who had been enemies of 'Uthman had their scruples about recognizing as Caliph one who, though not himself guilty, owed his accession in a large measure to

---

[106]Lewis, *The Arabs in History*, 48-49.

[107]Lewis, *The Arabs in History*, 50.

[108]Lewis, *The Arabs in History*, 59.

[109]Lewis, *The Arabs in History*, 59.

[110]Lewis, *The Arabs in History*, 60.

regicides....The opposition to him began with A'isha, Talha, and Zubayr....The triumvirate gathered forces for action against 'Ali and transferred themselves to Basra.... In October 656 'Ali marched out of Medina at the head of his forces. The event was doubly significant. In the first place, it marked the end of Medina as capital of the Islamic Empire.... In the second place, for the first time a Caliph was leading a Muslim army to civil war against brother Muslims.... From thence [Kufa] he marched against Basra and defeated the forces of the triumvirate in an engagement known as the "Battle of the Camel," since the main encounter took place around the camel on which A'isha, the "Mother of the Faithful," was riding....He was now master of the whole Islamic Empire, except for Syria, but despite his apparent strength his position was weakened by the tribal disunity and insubordination of his supporters and by the conflicting councils of the pietists who constituted a large part of his following and constantly challenged and questioned his authority."[111]

The struggle for power and legitimacy between 'Ali and Mu'awiya, the Meccan who was appointed ruler in Syria by 'Umar, and confirmed by 'Uthman, reverberates in Islam to this day. In it lies the seed of the ongoing Sunni-Shi'a political rift. Emerging from it has also come the ideological forebears of the modern jihadists, the Kharijites (or Khawarij).

Ostensibly secure on his throne, 'Ali from his new capital al-Kufah inaugurated his regime by dismissing most of the provincial governors appointed by his predecessor and exacting the oath of fidelity from the others....Mu'awiyah now came out as the avenger of the martyred Caliph [Uthman].... Withholding his homage from 'Ali, Mu'awiyah tried to corner him with this dilemma: Produce the assassins of the duly appointed successor of the Prophet or accept the position of an accomplice who is thereby disqualified from the Caliphate.... The real question was whether al-Kufah or Damascus, al-Iraq or Syria, should be supreme in Islamic affairs. Al-Madinah, which 'Ali had left soon after his installation in 656 never to revisit, was already out of the way. The weight of the far-flung conquests had shifted the centre of gravity to the north.... The final encounter took place on July 28, 657.... 'Ali's forces were on the point of victory when the shrewd, wily 'Amr ibn-al-As, Mu'awiyah's leader, resorted to a ruse. Copies of the Koran fastened to lances were suddenly thrust in the air — a gesture interpreted to mean an appeal from the decision of arms to the decision of the Koran. Hostilities ceased. Urged by his followers, the simple-hearted 'Ali accepted Mu'awiyah's proposal to arbitrate the case and thus spare Moslem blood. The arbitration was, of course, to be "according to the word of Allah" — whatever that may have meant.[112]

---

[111]Lewis, *The Arabs in History*, 61-62.
[112]Hitti, *History of the Arabs: From the Earliest Times to the Present*, 180-181.

What probably happened was that both referees deposed both principals, which left 'Ali the loser. Mu'awiyah had no Caliphate to be deposed from. He was but a governor of a province. The very fact of the arbitration itself had raised him to a level equivalent to that of 'Ali, whose position was thereby lowered to that of a mere pretender. The sentence of the judges deprived 'Ali of a real office, and Mu'awiyah of a fictitious claim which he had not yet dared publicly to assert. Not until 'Ali's death in 661, two years after the curtain on the arbitration farce, did Mu'awiyah's Caliphate receive general recognition.... The acceptance of the principle of arbitration proved disastrous to 'Ali in more ways than one: it alienated the sympathy of a large body of his followers. These Kharijites (seceders), as they were called, the earliest sect of Islam, proved his deadly foes. Adopting the slogan *la hukma illa li-l-Lah* (arbitration belongs to Allah alone), they rose in arms to the number of 4000....' Ali attacked their camp (659) and almost annihilated them, but they rose again under various names and remained a thorn in the side of the Caliphate till the 'Abbasid period.... Early on January 24, 661, as 'Ali was on his way to the mosque at al-Kufah, he was struck on the forehead with a poisoned saber. The weapon, which penetrated to the brain, was wielded by a Kharijite.[113]

With the death of 'Ali (661) what may be termed the republican period of the Caliphate, which began with abu-Bakr (632), came to an end. The four Caliphs of this era are known to Arab historians as *al-Rashidun* (orthodox). The founder of the second Caliphate, Mu'awiyah the Umayyad, a man of the world, nominated his son Yazid as his successor and thus became the founder of a dynasty. The hereditary principle was thereby introduced into the Caliphal succession never to be entirely abandoned.... The Umayyad Caliphate (661-750) with its capital at Damascus was followed by the 'Abbasid (750-1258) at Baghdad. The Fatimid Caliphate (909-1171), whose main seat was Cairo, was the only Shi'ite one of primary importance. Another Umayyad Caliphate at Cordova (Qurtubah) in Spain lasted from 929-1031. The last great Caliphate of Islam was non-Arab, that of the Ottoman Turks in Constantinople (*ca* 1517-1924).[114]

Three of the first four Caliphs were murdered. Muslim-on-Muslim violence, although some sought to uphold the Islamic principle that prohibits it, was enshrined early in Islam. This violence, which was brought to its "logical conclusion" at Karbala in 680, fueled the Shi'a (partisans of 'Ali) movement of Islam.

In 680 Yazid succeeded to the Caliphate without serious disturbance....His great misfortune arose from the development of events in Iraq...[where] the discontents of the Arabs with Syrian rule [had been aggravated] and led to a

---

[113]Hitti, *History of the Arabs: From the Earliest Times to the Present*, 182.
[114]Hitti, *History of the Arabs: From the Earliest Times to the Present*, 183-184.

movement in favor of Husayn, the son of 'Ali [and grandson of the Prophet].[115]

On the tenth day of the month of Muharram, at a place called Karbala in Iraq, Husayn, his family, and his followers encountered an Umayyad force and were ruthlessly put to death. Some seventy died in the massacre; only a sick boy, Ali ibn Husayn, who was left lying in a tent, survived. The dramatic martyrdom of the kin of the Prophet, and the wave of anguish and penitence that followed it, infused a new religious fervor in the Shi'a, now inspired by the potent themes of suffering, passion and expiation.[116]

The blood of al-Husayn, even more than that of his father, proved to be the seed of the Shi'ite "church." Shi'ism was born on the tenth of Muharram. From now on the imamship in 'Ali's progeny became as much of a dogma in the Shi'ite creed as that of the prophethood of Muhammad in Islam.[117]

Shi'a opposition to the Umayyad dynasty was based upon their support for the line of 'Ali. The Kharijites, on the other hand, did not support any hereditary succession, but felt that the old Arab tribal way of electing a leader should continue.

Arab-on-Arab (Muslim on Muslim) violence following the death of Yazid again opened a door for the Kharijites.

[W]ith the death of the Caliph Yazid in 683 revolts broke out among the Arabs, and inter-tribal warfare...gave Central Asia a respite from raids by the Arabs for several decades.... It should be noted that Khurasan, with Transoxiana, was not the only front on which the Arabs fought, for Sistan and the southern approaches to India were also part of the expansion in the east. In Sistan an additional problem was the gathering of Kharijites...who did not recognize the Umayyad Caliphate, and caused much fighting for Umayyad armies.[118]

Thus, the Kharijites opposed by force both 'Ali, and the victorious Umayyad Caliphate.

During the period between the death of the Prophet in 632 and the fall of the Umayyad Caliphate in 750 two [Shi'a and Kharijite] main heretical groups developed, expressing in religious terms the opposition of certain parties to the existing social and political order and to the orthodox faith that was its moral and public expression. One of these, the Kharijites, drew on largely Bedouin support and expressed resentment of the untamed nomads against the encroaching state — not so much against the Umayyad state specifically,

---

[115]Lewis, *The Arabs in History*, 68.

[116]Lewis, *The Assassins: A Radical Sect in Islam*, 22-23.

[117]Hitti, *History of the Arabs: From the Earliest Times to the Present*, 191.

[118] Richard N. Frye, *The Heritage of Central Asia: From Antiquity to Turkish Expansion* (Princeton, NJ: Markus Wiener Publishers, 2001), 207.

as against the very fact and notion of the state, of a constituted authority exercising constraint and even coercion and curtailing the total freedom of tribal society. The Kharijite theory of the Caliphate carries the doctrine of consent to the point of anarchy, and the Kharijites have indeed been described as the anarchist wing of the revolutionary opposition.[119]

Modern jihadists have been "tarred with the brush" of being "Kharijites." This claim stems from their failure to adhere to the dominance of established authority, their intolerance of fellow Muslims who disagree with them, and their ruthlessness and cruelty. An example of the application of Kharijite doctrine was the "Zanj" slave revolt of 869-883.

Though the leader of the Zanj claimed 'Alid descent he did not join the Shi'a, but rather the sect of the Kharijites, the egalitarian anarchists who had proclaimed in earlier times that the best man should be Caliph whatever his origins. In accordance with Kharijite doctrines the Zanj regarded all other Muslims as infidels, subject to slavery or the sword when captured.[120]

The Khawarij is one of the deviant sects that, among other errors, corrupted the rulings of Islam regarding warfare and Jihad to satisfy their evil beliefs and practices. They are called "Kwawarij" because their trademark was and still is open defiance (Khuruj) to Islamic Law, armed uprisings against Muslim Rulers and Communities, forming armed groups within Islamic states, causing mischief, and indiscriminate killing of civilians.[121]

Muslim Scholars consider the sects that follow their vain desires, and thus, defy the Prophet's Law and the consensus of Muslims, as being among the Khawarij, either literally, or by association of ideas and practices.[122]

Acts and beliefs of modern jihadists that lead to an association with the Khawarij by "association of ideas and practices" include:

The Khawarij do not abide by the Prophet's Sunnah regarding their ideas and practices; the Khawarij interpretation of the Quran is personal and based on previously formulated ideas, rather than modifying their ideas according to the Quran and Sunnah; they use general Quranic texts in a specific manner, while generalizing what is specific; they fight against each other and against other Muslims who do not agree with their ideas and practices; their trademark slogan and method is to rise against Muslim Rulers and to accuse Muslims who do not agree with them of being infidels; the Khawarij never participated in Jihad against non-Muslim aggressors...and never aided the Muslim Nation in performing true Islamic Jihad. Rather they always harm

---

[119]Lewis, *Islam in History*, 278.

[120]Lewis, *The Arabs in History*, 113.

[121]Abualrub, *Holy War Crusades Jihad: In the Torah, the Gospels, and the Quran*, 57.

[122]Abualrub, *Holy War Crusades Jihad: In the Torah, the Gospels, and the Quran*, 57.

Muslims, especially those who do not follow their ideas and deviant methods; even when the Khawarij attack non-Muslims, they do not follow the true rulings of the Quran and Sunnah regarding Jihad and warfare. Therefore, it is other Muslims who are harmed by the non-Islamic Jihad of the Khawarij. For example, and as a consequence of recent attacks that occurred in New York City and Washington, a worldwide campaign of oppression against every tenet of Islam and against Muslims in general was waged in the name of fighting terror; numerous prophetic statements refute the actions, ideas and behavior of the Khawarij; methods of modern-day Khawarij include committing suicide missions, hijackings, kidnappings and killing non-combatants, including women and children [However, we must state the difference between totally innocent non-combatants, and those who are a part of an aggressor nation or group]; they form armed gangs and so-called Jihadi groups that covertly operate within Islamic countries, in defiance of the governments that rule those countries; yet, an even bigger crime, is the fact that in the present time, the Khawarij have hijacked the just causes of Muslims in Palestine, Kashmir, Chechenya, the Philippines and the Balkans, who are suffering under brutal and bloody foreign occupations."[123]

According to their Muslim detractors, modern jihadists are in error, not because their aims are misguided, but because they follow the doctrine of the Kharijites. The proof of this is that Jihad has not been universally successful.

The just cause of Palestine, as well as principles of the true Islamic Jihad were lost in the midst of all the mischief caused by those who abandoned abiding by the Sunnah in times of war and conflict. They brought failure and defeat on the Palestinians, yet insist that their methods conform to true Jihad. Why is it then that they keep losing, even though Allah said in the Quran {O you who believe! If you help (in the cause of) Allah, He will help you, and make your foothold firm}? Therefore, if victory is delayed or if defeat occurs, it is because of the mistakes of Muslims, not because Allah lost his grip on the universe or broke His promise.[124]

Jihad, central to Islam, as the "instrument to transform the dar al-Harb into dar al-Islam,"[125] is recognized by the Kharijis as a guiding requirement in their religion. Fourteen hundred years later, Jihad appears as a permanent fixture of Islam, assuming the absence of a rapid collapse of the dar al-Harb to the forces of Jihad.

Jihadists don't teach their followers Islam; they indoctrinate them into Jihad. While Jihad is certainly a part of Islam, it is a small part of religious study, and perhaps the least complicated. Becoming an Islamic jurist is a lifetime endeavor, assuming that one can find suitable teachers. Jihad indoctrination is relatively quick, begun in Mosque discussions, and completed along

---

[123] Abualrub, *Holy War Crusades Jihad: In the Torah, the Gospels, and the Quran*, 59-67.

[124] Abualrub, *Holy War Crusades Jihad: In the Torah, the Gospels, and the Quran*, 68.

[125] Khadduri, *War and Peace in the Law of Islam*, 141.

with military training in relatively brief periods in training camps. The selected surahs that follow are among those most helpful for Jihad indoctrination.

Surah *Al-Baqarah* (the Heifer: The Qur'an provides a rich commentary of the glorious battles, and self sacrifice of early Islam. Key to the jihadists is reinforcing the belief that victory can be achieved against the odds. Surah [Qur'anic chapter] Al-Baqarah glorifies David over Goliath.

> Apart from the main lesson that if we would preserve our national existence and our faith it is our duty to fight with courage and firmness, there are other lessons in David's story: 1) numbers do not count, but faith, determination, and the blessing of Allah; 2) size and strength are of no avail against truth, courage, and careful planning; 3) the hero tries his own weapons, and those that are available to him at the time and place, even though they may laugh at him; 4) if Allah is with us, the enemy's weapon may become an instrument of his own destruction; 5) personality conquers all dangers, and puts heart into our wavering friends; 6) pure faith brings Allah's reward, which may take many forms: in David's case it was Power, Wisdom, and other gifts....[126]

Surah *Al-Imran* (the Family of Imran) glorifies martyrs, enjoins believers to remain resolute, and not to trust those outside of one's ranks. It emphasizes battles wherein Muslims gained victory although outnumbered.

> The Battle of Uhad was a great testing time for the young Muslim community. Their mettle and the wisdom and strength of their Leader were shown in the battle of Badr...in which the Makkan Pagans suffered a crushing defeat.... Had it not been for his firmness, courage, and coolness, all would have been lost. As it was, the Prophet, in spite of his wound, and many of the wounded Muslims, inspired by his example, returned to the field the next day, and Abu Sufyan and his Makkah army thought it was prudent to withdraw, Madinah was saved, but a lesson in faith, constancy, firmness, and steadfastness was learnt by the Muslims.[127]

"Uhad is as much a signpost for Islam as Badr. For the U.S. in these latter days it carries an even greater lesson. Allah's help will come if we have faith, obedience, discipline, unity, and the spirit of acting in righteousness and justice."[128] This Surah also provides comfort to the martyrs' families. "The Martyrs not only rejoice at the bliss they have themselves attained. The dear ones left behind are in their thoughts: it is part of their glory that they saved their dear ones from fear, sorrow, humiliation, and grief, in this life, even before they come to share in the glories of the Hereafter."[129] Of course, the Surah

---

[126] Abdullah Yusuf Ali, *The Meaning of the Holy Qur'an*, 9th ed. (Beltsville, MD: Amana Publications, 1998), 103.

[127] Ali, *The Meaning of the Holy Qur'an*, 159.

[128] Ali, *The Meaning of the Holy Qur'an*, 160.

[129] Ali, *The Meaning of the Holy Qur'an*, 172.

describes battles in which martyrs are created. The issue of the martyrdom of an Al-Qa'ida suicide bomber is not addressed.

Surah *Al-Nisa* (the Women) deals with the theme of "hypocrites" and continues the glorification of martyrs. Hypocrites to the jihadists are those so-called Muslims who disagree with them. Allah will overcome all odds. Unmentioned is the Surah that sets the requirement of a two-to-one strength ratio of Muslims against infidels, a function of Allah's awareness of human weakness.

> It is not everyone — least of all poltroons [utter cowards] and fainthearted persons — who is fit to fight in the cause of Allah [Jihad]. To do so is a privilege, and those who understand the privilege are prepared to sacrifice all their interests in this life, and this life itself; for they know that it is the sacrifice of something fleeting and of little value, for the sake of something everlasting, and of immense value. Whether (in appearance) they win or lose, in reality they win the prize for which they are fighting-viz., honour, and glory in the sight of Allah. Note that the only alternatives here are death or victory. The true fighter knows no defeat.[130]

> The courage of Muhammad was as notable as his wisdom, his gentleness, and his trust in Allah. Facing fearful odds, he often stood alone, and took the whole responsibility on himself. But his example and visible trust in Allah inspired and roused the Muslims and also — speaking purely from a human point of view — restrained the fury of his enemies. When we consider that he was Allah's inspired messenger to carry out His Plan, we can see that nothing can resist that Plan. If the enemy happens to have strength, power, or resources, Allah's strength, power, and resources are infinitely greater. If the enemy is meditating punishment on the righteous for their righteousness, Allah's punishment for such wickedness will be infinitely greater and more effective.[131]

Surah *Al-Anfa'l* (the spoils of war). The Jihad is not fought for personal gains, or spoils of war, but for the cause of Allah. Spoils, however, may be the result of this righteous fight. The jihadist should not be cowered by the odds against him. This surah does raise the possibility of peace, and the primacy of the imam in Jihad: "The purpose of this verse is to urge Muslims to act against the enemies described above [the Jewish Banu Qurayzah tribe] with a severity and resoluteness which would serve as a deterrent to other enemies of Islam who might be inclined to follow their example and act treacherously towards Muslims [Eds.]."[132]

> In the spring of 627 a Meccan army of some 10,000 men advanced to Medina and laid siege to the city. The simple expedient of digging a ditch [thus the

---

[130] Ali, *The Meaning of the Holy Qur'an*, 207.

[131] Ali, *The Meaning of the Holy Qur'an*, 211.

[132] Ali, *The Meaning of the Holy Qur'an*, 428.

battle's name of the Battle of the Trench] around it...was sufficient to defeat their siege-craft, and after forty days the army of Quraysh withdrew. This victory was followed by the destruction of the last remaining Jewish tribe, the Banu Qurayza, accused of intelligence with the Meccans. The men, according to the Sira, were put to death; the women and children sold into slavery.[133]3

There are always lurking enemies whom you may not know, but whom Allah knows. It is your duty to be ready against all, for the sacred Cause under whose banner you are fighting.[134]

Surah *Al-Tawbah* (The Repentance) or *Bara'ah* (The Disavowal), continues the theme of what to do about a "treacherous" violation of a treaty. It also decries the reluctance of some Muslims to participate in Jihad. "When war becomes inevitable, it must be prosecuted with vigor. According to the English phrase, you cannot fight with kid gloves. The fighting may take the form of slaughter or capture, or siege, or ambush or other stratagems. But even then there is room for repentance and amendment on the part of the guilty party, and if that takes place, our duty is forgiveness and the establishment of peace.... The repentance must be sincere, and that is shown by conduct — a religious spirit of true prayer and charity."[135]

Here is a good description of Jihad. It may require fighting in Allah's cause, as a form of self-sacrifice. But its essence consists in (1) a true and sincere Faith, which so fixes its gaze on Allah, that all selfish or worldly motives seem paltry and fade away, and (2) in earnest and ceaseless activity, involving the sacrifice (if need be) of life, person, or property, in the service of Allah. Mere brutal fighting is opposed to the whole spirit of Jihad, while the sincere scholar's pen or preacher's voice or wealthy man's contributions may be the most valuable forms of Jihad.[136]

Those who strive and suffer in Allah's cause are promised (1) a mercy specially for Himself, (2) His own good pleasure, (3) gardens of perpetual delight, (4) the supreme reward, Allah's own Presence or nearness.[137]

The choice is between two courses: will you chose a noble adventure and the glorious privilege of following your spiritual leader, or grovel in the earth for some small worldly gain or for fear of worldly loss?[138]

Selfish men think that charitable funds are fair game for raids, but the Islamic standards on this subject are very high.[139]

---

[133] Lewis, *The Arabs in History*, 42.

[134] Ali, *The Meaning of the Holy Qur'an*, 429.

[135] Ali, *The Meaning of the Holy Qur'an*, 438.

[136] Ali, *The Meaning of the Holy Qur'an*, 442.

[137] Ali, *The Meaning of the Holy Qur'an*, 443.

[138] Ali, *The Meaning of the Holy Qur'an*, 449.

[139] Ali, *The Meaning of the Holy Qur'an*, 455.

Surah *Al-Ahzab* (The Confederates): This surah continues the themes of treachery and cowardice, as exemplified in the "Battle of the Trench," and the inevitability of Allah's judgment and eventual victory.

> Before this year's [A.D. 627] mass attack on Madinah, the Muslims had successfully reached the Syrian border on the north, and were in hopes of reaching Yemen in the south. The Holy Prophet had seen signs of expansion and victory for the Muslims. Now that they were shut within the Trench on the defensive, the Hypocrites taunted them with having indulged in delusive hopes. But the event showed that the hopes were not delusive. They were realized beyond expectations in a few years.[140]

> The coward in a fight does not usually save himself from death. He is subject, after desertion, to the fury of the enemy and his own side for cowardice and desertion.... It is still worse if the cowardice or desertion is shown in a Cause, which because of the high issues of truth and justice may be called the Cause of Allah. How can anyone escape Allah's punishment?[141]

> The reference is to the Jewish tribe of Bani Qurayzah. They counted among the citizens of Madinah and were bound by solemn engagements to help in the defence of the city. But on the occasion of the Confederate siege by the Quraysh and their allies, they intrigued with the enemies and treacherously aided them.... The men of the Qurayzah were slain: the women were sold as captives of war: and their lands and properties were divided among the Muhajirs [holy warriors].[142]

Surah Muhammad or *Al Qital* (The Fighting) reinforces the necessity of fighting Jihad with determination and ferocity, even against those related to you who are supporting "evil." It condemns faint-heartedness and half measures.

> When once the fight (Jihad) is entered upon, carry it out with utmost vigor, and strike home your blows at the most vital points (smite at their necks), both literally and figuratively.[143]

> It is no use to say, as the Quraysh [Meccan tribe] said, that it is not seemly to fight against Kith and Kin. From one point of view the stand against sin brings "not peace, but a sword." It is a case of either subduing evil or being subdued by evil. If evil gets the upper hand, it is not likely to respect ties of Kith and Kin.[144]

---

[140] Ali, *The Meaning of the Holy Qur'an*, 1059.

[141] Ali, *The Meaning of the Holy Qur'an*, 1060.

[142] Ali, *The Meaning of the Holy Qur'an*, 1063-1064.

[143] Ali, *The Meaning of the Holy Qur'an*, 1315.

[144] Ali, *The Meaning of the Holy Qur'an*, 1321.

If we desert the Cause, the Cause will not fail. Better men than we will uphold the flag. But we should fall, and others will take our place, who are not so timid; half-hearted, or stingy.[145]

Surah *Al-Fatah* (The Victory). Patience leads to victory. Don't fight for booty, but for the cause.

This is best referred to the treaty of Hudaybiyah [the truce that Muhammad made with the Meccans]....In reality the door was then opened for the free spread of Islam throughout Arabia and thence the world.[146]

There may be neither fighting nor booty. But all who obey the righteous Imam's call to Jihad with perfect discipline will get the Rewards of the Hereafter.[147]

Surah *Al-Saff* (The Battle Array): Muslims should back their words with actions. This instruction attacks Israelites (Jews) and bolsters Muslims. It condemns Jews for not following Jesus.

The people of Moses often rebelled against him, vexed his spirit, and insulted him.... They did it not through ignorance, but from a selfish, perverse, and rebellious spirit, for which they received punishment. The Ummah of Islam [all Muslims] should remember and take note of it, and should avoid any deviation from the Law and Will of Allah."[148]

Over all religion: in the singular: not over all other religions in the plural. There is really only one true Religion, the Message of Allah, submission to the Will of Allah: this is called Islam. It was the religion preached by Moses and Jesus; it was the religion of Abraham, Noah and all the prophets, by whatever name it may be called. If people corrupt the pure light, and call their religions by other names, we must bear with them, and we may allow the names for convenience. But Truth must prevail over all.... If we seek Allah's help, we must first help Allah's cause, i.e., dedicate ourselves to Him entirely and without reserve.[149]

A portion of the Children of Israel — the one that really cared for the Truth — believed in Jesus and followed his guidance. But the greater portion of them were hard hearted, and remained in their beaten track of formalism and false racial pride. The majority seemed at first to have the upper hand when they thought they had crucified Jesus and killed the message. [150]

---

[145] Ali, *The Meaning of the Holy Qur'an*, 1325.

[146] Ali, *The Meaning of the Holy Qur'an*, 1328.

[147] Ali, *The Meaning of the Holy Qur'an*, 1333.

[148] Ali, *The Meaning of the Holy Qur'an*, 1460.

[149] Ali, *The Meaning of the Holy Qur'an*, 1462-1463.

[150] Ali, *The Meaning of the Holy Qur'an*, 1464.

As with all religious texts, it is the learned commentaries that provide the basis for religious jurisprudence. This review has covered only 9 of the 114 surahs in the Qur'an. It is therefore not nearly a complete analysis of Islam or the Qur'an. The commentary used, that of Abdullah Yusuf Ali, was published in English in Beltsville, Maryland. It is a commentary generally utilized throughout the U.S., and is provided to the U.S. Armed Forces. Therefore, it has been judged as being far from "radical." If a Muslim is inclined to place Jihad at the core of Islam, the above surahs certainly serve that purpose. It is not a "radical" reinterpretation of Islam that leads to Jihad, but rather an emphasis on Jihad as central to spreading the faith — and spreading the faith as central to Islam. Utilizing the same and/or additional surahs, it is likely that Al-Qa'ida teachers present a more radical interpretation than that described above.

Hatred for Jews can be discerned from the Qur'an, since Jewish tribes coexisted in Arabia during the time of Muhammad, and thus are included in his teachings. Hatred for the United States must, however, be derivative.

> There are...difficulties in the way of accepting imperialism as an explanation of Muslim hostility, even if we define imperialism narrowly and specifically, as the invasion and domination of Muslim countries by non-Muslims. If the hostility is directed against imperialism in that sense, why has it been directed so much stronger against Western Europe, which has relinquished all its Muslim possessions and dependencies, than against Russia, which still rules, with no light hand, over many millions of reluctant Muslim subjects and over ancient Muslim cities and countries? And why should it include the United States, which, apart from a brief interlude in the Muslim-minority area of the Philippines, has never ruled any Muslim population?...More to the point, it has not hitherto been the practice of the Soviets to quell disturbances with water cannon and rubber bullets, with TV cameras in attendance, or to release arrested persons on bail and allow them access to domestic and foreign media. The Soviets do not interview their harshest critics on prime time, or tempt them with teaching, lecturing, and writing engagements. On the contrary, their ways of indicating displeasure with criticism can often be quite disagreeable.[151]

This, of course, was written before the effects of the breakup of the Soviet Union were known. With the removal of "Soviet methods," Russia was faced with an Islamic civil war in Tajikistan, and is in its second war in Chechnya. The ultimate results of Russia's treating the Muslim populations of its empire in a "European manner" are yet to be seen.

> The cause most frequently adduced for anti-American feelings among Muslims today is American support for Israel. This support is certainly a factor of importance, increasing with nearness and involvement. But here again there are some oddities, difficult to explain in terms of a single simple cause. In the

---

[151]Lewis, "The Roots of Muslim Rage."

early days of the foundation of Israel, while the United States maintained a certain distance, the Soviet Union granted immediate *de jure* recognition and support, and arms sent from a Soviet satellite, Czechoslovakia, saved the infant state of Israel from defeat and death in its first weeks of life. Yet there seems to be no great ill will toward the Soviets for these policies, and no corresponding good will toward the United States. In 1956 it was the United States that intervened, forcefully and decisively, to secure the withdrawal of Israeli, British, and French forces from Egypt — in the late fifties and sixties it was to the Soviets, not America, that the rulers of Egypt, Syria, Iraq, and other states turned for arms; it was with the Soviet bloc that they formed bonds of solidarity at the United Nations and the world generally.[152]

The Soviet Union was near, and feared, but communism was not an ideological threat to Islam. The United States, as a non-imperialist power, was far away, and if it had to intervene in the region, as happened in World War Two, it was unlikely to stay. What is a danger to Islamists is the attractiveness of the "American way of life." Consumerism and personal freedom, especially the emancipation of women, pose the greatest threat to Islam since the days of Muhammad. Even the Mongols did not offer an attractive, alternative way of life, and were themselves converted to Islam. Couple the "American way of life" with the U.S. status as the sole world superpower, and the threat is immense and growing.

Jihadists hate the United States for what it represents, and not for what it does, or doesn't do. Thus the U.S. gets little or no credit when it aids Muslims, and often gets attacked for reasons having nothing to do with U.S. policies or actions.

And since the United States is the legitimate heir of European civilization and the recognized and unchallenged leader of the West, the United States has inherited the resulting grievances and become the focus for the pent-up hate and anger. Two examples may suffice. In November of 1979 an angry mob attacked and burned the U.S. Embassy in Islamabad, Pakistan. The stated cause of the crowd's anger was the seizure of the Grand Mosque in Mecca by a group of Muslim dissidents — an event in which there was no American involvement whatsoever. Almost ten years later, in February of 1989, again in Islamabad, the USIS center was attacked by angry crowds, this time to protest the publication of Salman Rushdie's *Satanic Verses*. Rushdie is a British citizen of Indian birth, and his book had been published five months previously in England. But what provoked the mob's anger, and also the Ayatollah Khomeini's subsequent pronouncement of a death sentence on the author, was the publication of the book in the United States.[153]

Often, this hatred goes beyond the level of hostility to specific interests or actions or policies or even countries, and becomes a rejection of Western

---

[152]Lewis, *"The Roots of Muslim Rage."*
[153]Lewis, *"The Roots of Muslim Rage."*

civilization as such, not so much for what it does as for what it is, and for the principles and values that it practices and professes. These are indeed seen as innately evil, and those who promote or accept them are seen as the "enemies of god."[154]

Even from a Muslim perspective that disagrees with Al-Qa'ida's version of Jihad, the West is still the aggrieving party.

Muslims were now permitted to attack pagans wherever they found them, since the persistent way and method of the pagans were blatant hostility against Muslims and Islam. Muslims did not have to wait for pagan attacks to retaliate, but were now permitted to preempt their aggression and seek to destroy them before they attack Muslims. In present times, the West leads a worldwide campaign of intimidation against its enemies and potential enemies. Western Countries send their navies cruising far away from their national shores; they also maintain strong naval presence in every water body in the world. They declare that their international water borders extend 72 nautical miles [sic], but send their navies to patrol within 12 nautical miles from the shore of other countries. They interfere in the affairs of nations far away from their borders and spy on every nation that exists on the earth. They believe that they are permitted to do so to protect their "national interests." However, they deny Muslims the same rights and lead an onslaught against every Islamic tenet, especially the true slogans of *Jihad*. Then, they act surprised when some Muslims retaliate, without permission from the Muslim Nation and in defiance of Islamic rules and the regulations governing *Jihad*; they ask, "Why do Muslims hate us?" To the contrary, it is Muslims who should ask the West, "Why do you hate us and seek to deprive us of our honor, religious freedom, the riches of our lands and the dream that all sincere Muslims have, to unite under the banner of one Islamic State?"[155]

The desire for a "pure Islamic State" (which has never existed) as an antidote to the West has found expression in Iran since the end of the 1970s, and more recently in the vision of Usama bin Laden.

From the lifetime of its Founder, and therefore in its sacred scriptures, Islam is associated in the minds and memories of Muslims with the exercise of political and military power. Classical Islam recognized a distinction between things of this world and things of the next, between pious and worldly considerations. It did not recognize a separate institution, with a hierarchy and laws of its own, to regulate religious matters. Does this mean that Islam is a theocracy? In the sense that God is seen as the supreme sovereign, the answer would have to be yes indeed. In the sense of government

[154]Lewis, *The Crisis of Islam*, 26.
[155]Abualrub, *Holy War Crusades Jihad: In the Torah, the Gospels, and the Quran*, 153-154.

by a priesthood, most definitely not. The emergence of a priestly hierarchy and its assumption of ultimate authority in the state is a modern innovation and is a unique contribution of the late Ayatollah Khomeini of Iran to Islamic thought and practice."[156]

Usama bin Laden presents the opposite picture to that of Ayatollah Khomeini, but with a like result. In fact, bin Laden presents a better "package" for an Islamic ruler. While Khomeini was a cleric who assumed political power, bin Laden is a businessman, victor in the Jihad against the Soviet Union, and general in the Jihad against America and the Jews, who is assuming clerical powers (as evidenced by the acceptance of his fatwas — see next section). Who better to assume the duties of a modern Caliph? Bin Laden, who was one of many who fought in the Afghan Jihad, and had training camps, has emerged as the "spiritual head" of global Jihad by his emphasis on spectacular operations and challenging Americans and Jews.

> If the peoples of the Middle East continue on their path, the suicide bomber may become a metaphor for the whole region, and there will be no escape from a downward spiral of hate and spite, rage and self-pity, poverty and oppression, culminating sooner or later in yet another alien domination; perhaps from a new Europe reverting to old ways, perhaps from a resurgent Russia, perhaps from some new, expanding superpower in the East.[157]

Perhaps from a non-imperialist United States forced to defend itself against unquenchable hate.

---

[156]Lewis, *The Crisis of Islam*, 20.
[157]Lewis, *What Went Wrong*, 159-160.

THE CALL TO JIHAD — THE CALL FOR GENOCIDE

Genocide is a strong word, and one that should not be used lightly, especially by an intelligence analyst. The word carries heavy baggage, evoking the image of Nazi Germany, the Holocaust, the organized murder of at least six million Jews, and others. The intelligence analyst, in invoking that term, bears a heavy burden. From a policy perspective, genocide cannot be ignored. From an intelligence perspective, declaring a situation genocide requires careful analysis, since it could easily drive policy. Conversely, failing to identify an ongoing genocide would be viewed as a major intelligence failure. Al-Qa'ida, and like-minded jihadists (but not all) are not at the point of the "Final Solution" to the "Jewish Question" that Nazi Germany reached from 1941-1945, but their policies vis-à-vis the Jewish people are genocidal. They follow their genocidal policy within the limits of their power, as did the Nazis from 1933 to 1941. When the Nazis gained control of large Jewish populations in Europe, power and opportunity combined to position the Nazis to harness the modern industrial state for the mass annihilation of a people. Al-Qa'ida's actions toward Jews are reminiscent of the continued violence perpetrated against Jewish communities within Nazi power from 1933 onward. Their level of anti-Jewish propaganda and population conditioning is similar to that of the Nazis. As in Nazi Germany, where ordinary Germans did not start out necessarily very anti-Semitic, but were conditioned by the government, the world's Muslim populations have been similarly conditioned as anti-Semites [the term here refers to anti-Jewish, not to be confused with Anti-Arab, who are also Semites]. Here again, Al-Qa'ida is executing a policy with broad Muslim support.

Anti-Semitism, as a result of the Holocaust, became very unfashionable in the West after World War Two. It lived on, however, in the Arab world (as a result of Arab-Jewish conflict in Palestine and later Israel, and the close relations between Arab leaders and Nazi Germany), and in the Soviet Union and its satellites in Eastern Europe. It was revived in Europe in the 1980s, and spread to the non-Arab Muslim world, in the guise of being anti-Israeli. This provided anti-Semites with the cover of criticizing Jews in their relation to and support of actions taken by the government of Israel in its conflict with the Palestinians, while denying that they are in fact anti-Semites. Although not all critics of Israeli government policy are anti-Semitic, the real anti-Semites were provided a broad tent under which to hide and grow. In the 1990s, and currently, Jews are being attacked and killed without regard to their position with respect to supporting the actions of the government of Israel. A severe example of this was the 1994 bombing of the Jewish Cultural Center and school in Buenos Aires, Argentina. The children in that school were killed because they were Jews, not because of any connection to Israel. Al-Qa'ida, only recently paying lip service to the Palestinian cause, does not differentiate between Israelis and Jews. Islam, recognizing no separation of state and religion, views Israel as a "state" of Jews (which is recognized by few Arab governments and not at all by Islamists/jihadists), just as the United States is viewed as a Christian state. Al-Qa'ida did not declare Jihad against Israel, but against Jews.

On February 23, 1998, *Al-Quds al-'Arabi*, an Arabic newspaper in London, printed the full text of a "Declaration of the World Islamic Front for Jihad Against the Jews and the Crusaders." According to the paper, the statement was faxed to them, with the signatures of Usama bin Ladin and the leaders of Jihad groups in Egypt, Pakistan, and Bangladesh.... The facts, it says, are known to everyone and set forth under three main headings.... First — for more than seven years the United States is occupying the lands of Islam in the holiest of its territories, Arabia, plundering its riches, overwhelming its rulers, humiliating its people, threatening its neighbors, and using its bases in the peninsula as a spearhead to fight against the neighboring Islamic peoples.... Second — despite the immense destruction inflicted on the Iraqi people at the hands of the Crusader Jewish alliance, and in spite of the appalling number of dead, exceeding a million, the Americans nevertheless, in spite of all this, are trying once more to repeat this dreadful slaughter.... Third — while the purposes of the Americans in these wars are religious and economic, they also serve the petty state of the Jews, to divert attention from their occupation of Jerusalem and their killing of Muslims in it.... These crimes, the statement goes on to say, amount to a "clear declaration of war by the Americans against God, His Prophet, and the Muslims. In such a situation, it is the unanimous opinion of the ulema throughout the centuries that when enemies attack the Muslim lands, Jihad becomes a personal duty of every Muslim."[158]

While the fatwa is obviously directed mainly against the United States, two of the three "grievances" include a connection to "the Jews," as does the title.

After citing some further relevant Qur'an verses, the document continues: "By God's leave, we call on every Muslim who believes in God and hopes for reward to obey God's command to kill the Americans and plunder their possessions wherever he finds them and whenever he can. Likewise we call on the Muslim ulema and leaders and youth and soldiers to launch attacks against the armies of the American devils and against those who are allied with them from among the helpers of Satan."[159]

Does being anti-Semitic and attacking Jews rise to the level of a policy of genocide? Genocide is a policy. The Holocaust was the nearly successful execution of that policy that resulted in millions of deaths. A Holocaust does not have to occur for there to be a genocidal policy. Conversely, the death of a large number of people, in and of itself, does not necessarily constitute genocide. Following World War Two, on 9 December 1948, the United Nations promulgated a very broad definition of genocide:

Any of the following acts committed with the intent to destroy in whole or in part, a national, ethnical, racial or religious group, as such: a. Killing members

---

[158]Lewis, *The Crisis of Islam*, xxiv-xxvi.
[159]Lewis, *The Crisis of Islam*, xxvii.

of the group. b. Causing serious bodily or mental harm to members of the group. c. Deliberately inflicting on the group conditions of life calculated to bring about its physical destruction in whole or in part. d. Imposing measures intended to prevent births within the group. e. Forcibly transferring children of the group to another group.[160]

Under this very expansive definition, hundreds of international conflicts can, and have, been declared to be genocide. The phrase "intent to destroy in whole or in part" makes the definition useless. In any conflict there is always an intent to destroy at least in part. The specific description of the actions taken to constitute genocide are also overly broad: "killing a member of the group" is an example. Under this definition it is easy, and wrong, to declare Al-Qa'ida a genocidal organization. That does not mean, however, that it is not such an organization. A more restrictive, and accurate definition is: "Genocide is a form of one-sided mass killing in which a state or other authority intends to destroy a group, as that group and membership in it are defined by the perpetrator."[161] The only modification necessary to this definition is that the intent is to destroy that group "wherever it may be found" and that members of the group cannot "opt out," since membership is defined by the perpetrator. The more restrictive definition excludes situations of what is now called "ethnic cleansing" in which the intent is not the elimination of a people or group, but their departure from a particular area. Al-Qa'ida cannot, under Islam, settle for the U.S.'s leaving Saudi Arabia (as we will soon find out), nor can they settle for Jews leaving Israel. Islam certainly has, and does, tolerate Judaism as a "religion of the book," with adherents under Islamic "protection" as dhimmis. Modern Islamic/jihadist concepts, and Al-Qa'ida practice, have evolved into genocidal policies toward Jews. The anti-Semitism of 19th-century France was more virulent than that of 19th-century Germany. It was in Germany, however, in which in the 20th Century the conditions were created to intensify anti-Semitism, and evolve it into the Holocaust. This stance has been adopted in Arab Islam, and is being spread to Muslims globally. Hatred of Jews is endemic in the Middle East, and provides a willing environment for Al-Qa'ida to call for the killing of Jews.

It has been said that the peoples of Europe, especially those of Eastern Europe, received anti-Semitism in "their mother's milk," i.e., it was inculcated in the children from an early age. The same process, transferred from Europe, has been occurring in the Arab world for the past several decades.

Another European contribution to this debate [stemming from Muslims asking: Who did this to us?] is anti-Semitism, and blaming "the Jews" for all that goes wrong. Jews in traditional Islamic societies experienced the normal constraints and occasional hazards of minority status.... With rare exceptions, where hostile stereotypes of the Jew existed in Muslim tradition, they tended

---

[160]Frank Chalk and Kurt Jonassohn, *A History and Sociology of Genocide* (New Haven, CT: Yale University Press, 1990), 10.

[161]Chalk and Jonassohn, *A History and Sociology of Genocide*, 23.

to be contemptuous and dismissive rather than suspicious and obsessive. This made the events of 1948 — the failure of five Arab states and armies to prevent half a million Jews from establishing a state in the debris of the British Mandate for Palestine — all the more of a shock.... Anti-Semitism and its demonized picture of the Jew as a scheming, evil monster provided a soothing answer.... [F]rom 1933 Nazi Germany and its various agencies made a concerted and on the whole remarkably successful effort to promote and disseminate European style anti-Semitism in the Arab world. The struggle for Palestine greatly facilitated the acceptance of the anti-Semitic interpretation of history, and led some to blame all evil in the Middle East and indeed in the world on secret Jewish plots. This interpretation has pervaded much of the public discourse in the region, including education, the media, and even entertainment.[162]

Anti-Semitism has become so rooted in Arab culture that a book written to counter the interpretation of Islam by Al-Qa'ida and other jihadists is permeated with an anti-Semitic world view. It is both ironic, and telling of the depth of anti-Semitism in Muslim society, that those who present the case against Al-Qa'ida, which requires no discussion of Jews, unless, of course, to condemn the targeting of these "people of the book" and innocents, in fact reinforces Al-Qa'ida's genocidal practices:

The Jewish religion is a racist religion that is inherited from mother to children; the Jews neither preach Judaism to other than Jews, nor do they encourage converting to Judaism.... The Jews consider themselves to be the children of God and His chosen people; they do not believe in any other religion, especially Islam.[163]

Of course, as mentioned earlier, the Wahabbis who control Saudi textbooks cite the Koran in stating: "never will Jews or the Christians be satisfied with you unless you follow their form of religion." Jews are thus vilified for not encouraging conversions to Judaism, but also for insisting upon it. Anti-Semitism is never rooted in logic, but in hatred.

In discussing the Islamic prohibition against the killing of innocents, hatred for Jews is quite evident, and prohibiting attacks on "innocent" Jews is made with reluctance, and in a footnote.

However, we must state the difference between totally innocent non-combatants, and those who are part of an aggressor nation or group. While Islam prohibits the killing of non-combatants, as we will soon prove, it does not mean that all non-combatants are "innocent." For example, we mention the herds of Americans who claim to be Jews, especially the women from Brooklyn, who, as compared to many Israeli Jews — and even radical elements in the Israeli government, are far more radical in their enmity to Muslims and Arabs, even Christian Arabs. They migrate to Palestine, forcibly settle on lands owned by Arabs, engage in clear hostile acts against them

[162]Lewis, *What Went Wrong*, 153-154.

[163]Abualrub, *Holy War Crusades Jihad: In the Torah, the Gospels, and the Quran*, 94.

and frequently call for the expulsion of Arabs from their own homeland. Indeed, these are by no means "innocent." However, and as much as these people are hated because of their wickedness and viciousness in stealing land that does not belong to them, Muslims are required to refrain from attacking non-combatants. Also, by saying "Muslims" here, we are exclusively referring to Muslim Leaders, the only authority to declare war, lead its operations and conduct peace, as we will soon prove.[164]

Your honor, I demand a new lawyer!

Even when accusing Al-Qa'ida of being Khawariji (an early fundamentalist Islamic sect), Jews cannot not be left out of the argument.

> Among the early armed conflicts started by the Khawarij, is the crimes of uprising against and then the murder of the third Caliph, 'Uthman ibn 'Affan, may Allah be pleased with him. They also fought against Ali ibn Abi Talib, the fourth Caliph, and assassinated him, may Allah be pleased with him. During the era under discussion, the Khawarij led to a major conflict in the Muslim World and were especially eager to shed the blood of the Prophet's companions, who transferred Islam to them. For more details about the murders of 'Uthman and Ali and the role played by the Khawarij and Jews in their murders, refer to the major book of Islamic history, *al-Bidayah wan-Nihayah* (The Beginning and the End), by Imam ibn Kathir.[165]

The Muslim expulsion from Spain after its reconquest by the Christians (1492) is currently viewed as a major grievance of Islam against Christianity, although not seen as a large calamity at the time. The Jews were also a victim of an expulsion and later the Spanish Inquisition. While describing this shared victimization at the hands of the Spanish monarchy, a footnote cannot help but attack today's Jews: "In Palestine, the Jews are now enthusiastically 'paying back' Muslim generosity and hospitality that lasted for eight centuries in Muslim Spain and for several more centuries in the rest of the Muslim World."[166]

The establishment of a Jewish homeland in the British mandate of Palestine is viewed as the cause of the problems of the Muslim world.

> Europe succeeded in finding a final solution [an interesting phrase!] for European and world Jews, by engaging them in a battle they cannot win against more than twelve hundred million Muslims who consider all of Palestine their property and Holy Land. Further, the Arabs were forced to engage in a war of attrition against the Jews, backed by the collective strength of the world of Christendom, thus delaying their integration into one nation, severely limiting

---

[164]Abualrub, *Holy War Crusades Jihad: In the Torah, the Gospels, and the Quran*, 65-66.

[165]Abualrub, *Holy War Crusades Jihad: In the Torah, the Gospels, and the Quran*, 62.

[166]Abualrub, *Holy War Crusades Jihad: In the Torah, the Gospels, and the Quran*, 148.

their economies and curtailing their military, industrial, scientific and social advancements.[167]

In other words, the Europeans have forced the Muslims to kill the Jews, which they will eventually do.

Another anti-Semitic theme that has emerged in the Muslim world, and that has been boosted in Europe, is that it is now the Jews who have become the "Nazis" and are perpetrating a Holocaust against the Palestinians. It is easy to see the value of this view to Arab propaganda drumming up hatred to Jews. It is less obvious, but equally easy to understand why Europeans, burdened with their own guilt over a true Holocaust, take solace in viewing their former victims as current perpetrators.

> The Jews are now inventing a Holocaust of their own against Palestinian Muslims and Christians. They once again misused the hospitality offered them by Arabs, who tolerated their presence in Palestine during the early part of the last century when Jews were being slaughtered in Europe. The Jews committed similar mistakes during the time of the Prophet of Islam, peace be upon him, by betraying the peace pacts they conducted with Arab Muslims."[168]

Jewish Holocaust denial is a familiar theme among Arabs and jihadists. A different twist on the theme is the minimization of the Jewish Holocaust relative to the vast number of deaths that occurred in WWII. What is missed in this analysis is the difference between a true genocide and the death of large numbers of people during the course of a conflict. As a well-thought-out definition of genocide shows, the number of deaths, although a tragedy, does not indicate genocide.

> The Jews dwell on calling their predicament at the hands of Western Europe before and during the Second World War, "The Holocaust." However, it should be known that many nations suffered extreme losses during this war, such as hundreds of thousands of Muslim casualties in Central Europe, North Africa, Southeast Asia, etc. Russia and China lost millions of civilian and military casualties under German and Japanese occupation, respectively. However, the Jews cried louder and longer regarding the atrocities directed against them, to play on the sympathy of Christian Europe so that the West supports its bloody and illegal occupation of Palestine. Thus, the West atoned for its sins by granting the Jews a land that did not belong to them and caused the displacement of millions of innocent Palestinians. It seems that Christians pretend that Jewish blood, which they spilled and shed throughout their history, is worth more than Muslim and Arab blood. The Jews should know better.[169]

---

[167] Abualrub, *Holy War Crusades Jihad: In the Torah, the Gospels, and the Quran*, 231.
[168] Abualrub, *Holy War Crusades Jihad: In the Torah, the Gospels, and the Quran*, 249-250.
[169] Abualrub, *Holy War Crusades Jihad: In the Torah, the Gospels, and the Quran*, 263.

The same ideological interpretation of Islam that brings us Al-Qa'ida, also brings anti-Semitism.

> A key figure in the development of these new attitudes [anger at and contempt for America] was Sayyid Qutb, an Egyptian who became a leading ideologue of Muslim fundamentalism and an active member of the fundamentalist organization known as the Muslim Brotherhood. Born in a village in Upper Egypt in 1906, he studied in Cairo and for some years worked as a teacher and then as an official in the Egyptian Ministry of Education.[170]

> He [Qutb] devoted a separate book, published posthumously in Saudi Arabia, to "our battle with the Jews": *Ma'rakatuna ma'a al-Yahud* (Jedda, 1970). In addition to the specific Arab conflict with the Jews, he speaks of the pernicious Jewish role in the war against Islam and more generally against religious values: "Behind the atheist, materialist conception is a Jew — [Marx]; behind the bestial sexual conception, a Jew [Freud]; behind the destruction of the family and the disruption of the holy bonds of society, a Jew — [Durkheim]." The three are actually named not by Sayyid Qutb but by his editor, who for good measure adds a fourth in a footnote-Jean-Paul Sartre, made into a Jew for this purpose, as the inspirer of the literature of disintegration and ruin. It seems likely that Sayyid Qutb's inspiration for this and other anti-Jewish (as distinct from anti-Israel and anti-Zionist) passages was European or American.[171]

The hatred runs deep, and is inculcated throughout their lives. For most Arabs, and frequently most Muslims, there is no difference between Israelis and Jews. In fact, their historic refusal to acknowledge the existence of a state called Israel has made the existence of an "Israeli" an impossibility. The Muslims are thus left with describing the antagonists of the Arab Palestinians as either Zionists, or more often just Jews. Just as in Europe where there has emerged a modern phenomenon of anti-Semitism without Jews, so it is the case first in the Arab world and now more broadly in the Muslim world, even in countries where there has never been a Jewish population. Thus, in Indonesia, the most populous Muslim country, the jihadists have developed an anti-Semitic streak. Abu Bakar Ba'asyir, a leading Indonesian jihadist, was arrested following the Bali bombings on suspicion of involvement in terrorist activities and of being the spiritual leader of Jemaah Islamiyah (JI). Ba'asyir also was one of the founders of a non-governmental organization called the Council of Indonesian Mujahidin (*Majelis Mujahidin Indonesia*, MMI).

> Ba'asyir does speak regularly and in blanket terms of the moral bankruptcy of the Indonesian state. He preaches the absolute and unique veracity of "Islam," and of the need to promote it in society. He rejects the legitimacy of the secular state out of hand. But he goes further than simple, strident moral absolut-

---

[170]Lewis, *The Crisis of Islam*, 76-77.
[171]Lewis, *The Crisis of Islam*, 169.

ism. His political analysis travels far into the realm of conspiracy theory in which Indonesian Christianity, together with a cartoonishly drawn cabal of Jews/Zionists/Israelis/Mossad, combine to divide, corrupt, and undermine Muslims and Islam. A similarly deep vein of anti-Semitism is found in the ideas of other leading members of MMI, particularly its functional chief, Irfan Awwas.[172]

Just as in the waning days of World War II when a defeated and isolated Hitler in his bunker continued to divert precious resources better used to support combat to killing Jews, Usama bin Laden is showing his true colors by lashing out from hiding. In a 14 February 2003 message to Muslims, credited to bin Laden, he said:

> Therefore, I advise the youths to exercise their minds in the Jihad as they are the first ones upon whom Jihad is obligatory.... So know that targeting the Americans and the Jews [not Israelis or Zionists] by killing them in any corner of the Earth, is the greatest of obligations and the most excellent of ways to gain nearness to Allah. Furthermore, I advise the youths to use their intelligence in killing them secretly.[173]

Just as the Hitler Youth, indoctrinated from a young age by the Nazis, defended Berlin in its death throes, Islamic youth, indoctrinated in Jihad in countless *madrassas* (schools for Muslim scholars), are called upon to kill the "enemies" of Islam from bin Laden's "bunker."

The importance of killing Jews, as opposed to just Americans, is emphasized in the January 2002 kidnapping and subsequent murder of *Wall Street Journal* reporter Daniel Pearl, in Pakistan, by local jihadists with Al-Qa'ida ties. In the video of his beheading, Pearl is forced to confirm that both sets of his grandparents were Jewish. Thus, by all branches of Judaism, he would be recognized as a Jew. This was not Pearl affirming his Jewish faith; it was the jihadists affirming the permissibility of beheading him under shari'a. Being an American was not enough; he was a Jew.

---

[172]Tim Behrend, "The Public Teachings of Abu Bakar Ba'asyir," *Ambon PosKo Zwolle,* online ed., in English, 26 May 2003, URL: <*https://datawarehouse10.dia.ic.gov/fcgi-bin/webisdoc*>, accessed 29 May 2003.

[173]Yossef Bodansky, "Osama Bin Ladin and the New Crusader War: Bin Laden's New Secret Message to the Islamist Leadership," *Defense and Foreign Affairs Daily,* online ed., 20 February 2003, 10.

DEPROGRAMMING THE JIHADISTS: CAN IT BE DONE?

Millions of Muslim youth have been taught to hate. They have been taught a severe, although not necessarily illegitimate, version of their religion. While "public" school systems throughout the Arab, and likely the Muslim world, contain elements of anti-Western and anti-Semitic studies, there are millions of Muslim youths in madrassas in Pakistan, Yemen, India, and elsewhere who are taught little else but Jihad. These schools flourish because those states do not provide an affordable education, and jihadists fund these private madrassas, providing free education.

Upon completion of studies at these "schools" the student is prepared for no employment other than Jihad, or teaching Jihad. Millions are attending, or have graduated, such institutions. They believe in their cause, and may be expected to act upon those beliefs if given the opportunity. Eliminating this aspect of the threat will be a time-consuming, expensive, and daunting task. A similar dilemma faced the victorious allies as they approached the end of the Second World War in Europe and came to grips with what to do with Nazism.

The issue facing President Franklin D. Roosevelt, his administration, and later President Harry S. Truman, was addressable as two questions. What surrender terms, if any, would be offered Nazi Germany, and how could Germany be "de-Nazified"? To Roosevelt the issues were related, in that Germany must be treated in a way that would preclude a post-war situation in which Germany would again emerge to threaten the world. As Assistant Secretary of the Navy in the First World War, Roosevelt had stated that: "The one lesson the German will learn is the lesson of defeat."[174] By the Second World War, Roosevelt realized that simply defeating Germany was not enough. The very worldview that led the Germans to start two world wars must be changed. At the January 1943 Casablanca Conference with Churchill, Roosevelt not only enunciated his much-debated "unconditional surrender" policy toward Germany, Italy and Japan, but more tellingly said "the Allies would fight to destroy 'the philosophies in those countries which are based on conquest and the subjugation of other people.'"[175] At the November 1943 Tehran Conference, with Stalin in attendance in addition to Churchill, Roosevelt told both leaders that it was "very important not to leave in the German mind the concept of 'the Reich.'...The very word should be stricken from the language."[176] At the same meeting the leaders discussed the draconian measures that may have to be taken to de-Nazify Germany. Stalin, being Stalin, and not shy from dealing with issues of killing large numbers of people, suggested that 50,000 Nazis would have to be killed. Churchill insisted that only "war criminals" need be killed. Roosevelt replied in jest "say 49,500."[177] In a Christmas 1943 radio address to

---

[174]Michael Beschloss, *The Conquerors: Roosevelt, Truman and the Destruction of Hitler's Germany, 1941-1945* (New York: Simon and Schuster, 2002), 11.

[175]Beschloss, *The Conquerors: Roosevelt, Truman and the Destruction of Hitler's Germany*, 14.

[176]Beschloss, *The Conquerors: Roosevelt, Truman and the Destruction of Hitler's Germany*, 24.

[177]Beschloss, *The Conquerors: Roosevelt, Truman and the Destruction of Hitler's Germany*, 27.

the American people, Roosevelt said that the allies had "no intention to enslave the German people" but to "rid them once and for all of Nazism and Prussian militarism and the fantastic and disastrous notion that they constitute the 'Master Race.'"[178] In August 1944 Roosevelt said: "We have got to be tough with the German people — not just the Nazis. You either have to castrate the German people or you have got to treat them in such a manner so they can't just go on reproducing people who want to continue the way they have in the past."[179] When his Secretary of the Treasury, Henry Morgenthau Jr., told Roosevelt that the "other big problem" [in addition to German industry] was "Germans between twenty and forty who had been inculcated with Nazism," Roosevelt said, "You will have to create entirely new textbooks for the Germans."[180]

In October 1944, when American troops entered Germany: "Eisenhower's Proclamation Number One 'to the people of Germany' began, 'The Allied forces serving under my command have now entered Germany. We come as conquerors, but not as oppressors. In the area of Germany occupied by the forces under my command, we shall obliterate Nazism and German militarism.'"[181] On 10 May 1945 President Truman signed Joint Chiefs of Staff Directive 1067, which ordered the commander of the American zone to denazify, demilitarize and reeducate the Germans.[182]

Just as World War Two was the result of an underlying German militancy and Nazi concept of the "master race," modern Jihad has emerged from a Muslim history of global expansion and conquest, underpinned by a religion claiming to represent the only "truth." Islam was established by Mohammad as a religion of conquest. Thus, when modern jihadists look toward the "roots" of their religion, they find a drive to global expansion. What they fail to find is the history of Islam that has tempered that early drive with rules of Jihad that recognize the power relationships in the real world that has constrained Islam's military expansion. They, in essence, reject the rules of Jihad that don't suit their purpose. While the West waits, and hopefully attempts to establish the conditions for a reformation of Islam that will allow for that great religion to coexist with all religions, a "reeducation" of jihadists, similar in design, but larger in scope, to the denazification of Germany, will be necessary. It involves both the "deprogramming" of current jihadists, and the elimination of future jihadists through a rewriting of the textbooks that breed intolerance and conflict.

Central to jihadist "deprogramming" is their limited knowledge of their own religion. In most instances even the operational leadership of Al-Qa'ida and other jihadist groups are not Islamic jurists. They have learned a very narrow, and unscholarly, version of Islam that emphasizes Jihad, but not the intricacies of the laws of Jihad. Their

---

[178]Beschloss, The Conquerors: Roosevelt, Truman and the Destruction of Hitler's Germany, 34.

[179]Beschloss, The Conquerors: Roosevelt, Truman and the Destruction of Hitler's Germany, 85.

[180]Beschloss, The Conquerors: Roosevelt, Truman and the Destruction of Hitler's Germany, 100.

[181]Beschloss, The Conquerors: Roosevelt, Truman and the Destruction of Hitler's Germany, 159.

[182]Beschloss, The Conquerors: Roosevelt, Truman and the Destruction of Hitler's Germany, 233.

recruits, therefore, are susceptible to counter-indoctrination by learned jurists in a controlled environment.

Such a program is reported to be having success in Yemen. The Yemeni government established a program inside the prisons of Yemeni Intelligence for 104 men detained on charges of belonging to Al-Qa'ida. The detainees were broken into small 5-7 men discussion groups and assigned to committee members who specialized in the given subject matter.

> Judge Hammud al-Hattar, a member of the High Court who headed the Dialogue Committee, elucidated the experiment.... He said the conclusion reached was that the problem of these detainees was due to their reliance on the memorization of texts without apprehension of the real situations on which these texts apply. The youths do not know the procedures for deducing Shari'a rules on the basis of stringent requirements, and they apply fetwas issued by individuals who are not fit to perform Ifta issuance of fetwas. He said the concepts they harbor came originally from outside Yemen....The committee followed a number of principles in this dialogue. These were defining the subjects of debate in advance, studying the issues under discussion and tracing them to their Shari'a roots and the relevant references. There was also a utilization of the documents of the religious group Islamic in Egypt which were published in four books. There was commitment to listening to the other party, respect for the views expressed and friendly persuasion and responding to argument with counter-argument.... The acknowledged principles in deducing Shari'a rules on the basis of proper postulates were exercised to reach an orthodox understanding of Islam's dictates.[183]

The agreements reached with the detainees were based upon the concept of the primacy of the Muslim Ruler, now head of a Muslim state, in declaring Jihad and issuing *aman* (safe-conduct). Although the jihadists under Sunni Islam ought to accept the state as legitimate, should they not, then the premise of the agreement is invalid. According to Al-Hattar:

> Concerning those we had the debate with, we have elevated them to the required level and the results were good.... These can be summarized in firstly the mandatory obedience to those in charge and commitment to the Constitution and the laws in force.... Secondly: Preserving the country's stability and refraining from any action that undermines its security. Thirdly: Respecting the rights of...non-Muslims and those covered by treaties or given a pledge of safety. This includes the inviolability of their blood, possessions and honor. Fourthly: Not touching or targeting the embassies and interests of the nations that have treaties with the Yemen Republic as long as

---

[183]"We Have Voided the Bases of Bin-Ladin's Fetwas," *London Al-Majallah*, in Arabic, 23 February 2003 through 02 March 2003, 26-28

the pledge lasts. Permission to enter the country is considered a pledge of safety for anybody who gets it, until it is cancelled by a decision from the relevant authority.... So far 36 persons not accused of criminal offenses have been released. The rest are to be released consecutively.[184]

The four books referred to by Al-Hattar were published by the leaders of al-Jama'a al-Islamiyya in 2002 while in Egyptian jails.

> Egyptian authorities allowed the historical leaders to tour Egyptian prisons in the spring and summer of 2002 so they could explain the initiative [calling for nonviolence] to their followers. Finally, in 2002 the historical leaders published four books that use shari'a to refute the legitimacy of armed Islamist struggle and to justify nonviolence. These books have been widely distributed in Egypt. To dispel any doubts about whether the books represent the position of al-Jama'a al-Islamiyya, each of the four volumes lists the names of those who researched and wrote it, as well as those who reviewed and approved it. The names include all the historical leaders."[185]

The books, however, do not repudiate Jihad as applicable in modern times. They instead take the shari'a view that a Muslim shouldn't fight if they can't win. The corollary, of course, is to wait until one is strong enough, and then attack. The books, as shown in the Yemeni example, are useful in blunting modern jihadists.

> [In] [t]he first book....The authors argue that the shari'a foundation for the initiative is the principle of interest. The initiative is in the interest of al-Jama'a al-Islamiyya and of the Muslim umma, enabling both to avoid the dangers of *fitna* (sedition). Conversely, the continuation of armed struggle would serve the interests of Islam's enemies, which the author's list as Israel, the United States, and secularist intellectuals in Muslim countries. The authors also claim that violence against Muslims and non-Muslims alike is prohibited by Islamic shari'a for multiple reasons, even if undertaken in the name of Jihad. First, Jihad is prohibited if it is unlikely to attain its goal, or if it becomes an obstacle to the peaceful preaching of Islam. Second, Jihad is prohibited if those who are intent on undertaking it are incapable of waging it successfully. Third, it is harmful to the umma if there are Muslims among the non-Muslims whose lives could be endangered by the fighting. Fourth, Islam prohibits Jihad against monotheists, for example, Jews and Christians, who are willing to live peacefully with Muslims; Islam also prohibits fighting against those who have not been exposed to Islam. Finally, Jihad is prohibited if the harm it causes is greater than the benefits obtained for the umma, or if peace has been established.... It is worth noting that the first volume also reveals that there

---

[184]"We Have Voided the Bases of Bin-Ladin's Fetwas," 26-28.

[185]Mustapha Kamel Al-Sayyid, "The Other Face of the Islamist Movement," Working Papers, *Carnegie Endowment for International Peace*, Global Policy Program, Democracy and Rule of Law Project, no. 33, January 2003, 16.

was initial disagreement about the initiative between al-Jama'a al-Islamiyya leaders in Egypt and those abroad. According to the book, the latter opposed the initiative in 1997 and 1998; in 1999 all the leaders finally resolved to endorse nonviolence.[186]

The Egyptian Al-Gama'at al-Islamiyya has its largest presence outside Egypt in Italy...They are associated primarily with the Islamic Cultural Institute of Milan and the Islamic Tuscan Community of Florence.[187]

In interviews, the historical leaders also explained that during two decades of imprisonment, they had plenty of time to rethink their strategies and examine their compatibility with shari'a principles.... They also examined the work of thirteenth-century Muslim scholars such as Ibn Taymiyya in historical context and concluded that his confrontation with the Mongols in the thirteenth century was very different from their own relationship to the Muslim rulers of a Muslim state in the twentieth century.[188]

The initial reluctance of the external leadership may have stemmed from the fact that it was obviously easier to continue the violent Jihad from the comfort of Europe than from an Egyptian jail.

The second book flows directly from the first, listing the errors committed by al-Jama'a al-Islamiyya in its armed confrontation with the government.... The authors of the book declare that the views of Muslim scholars from the past may be adapted to changing conditions and times, implicitly distancing themselves from the views articulated by Muslim scholars in the thirteenth century, such as Ibn Taymiyya [a great influence on Wahhabism]. The authors explain that Jihad, properly understood, is a means to an end and not an end in itself. Muslims should not undertake Jihad in cases where they are likely to fail. Additionally, they declare that shari'a forbids the murder of persons who do not take part in military operations against Islam or do not obstruct the peaceful preaching of Islam. The authors explicitly address the issue of foreign tourists [this group killed 60 foreign tourists in Luxor in 1997, causing considerable damage to the Egyptian tourist industry], declaring that Muslims must protect tourists who use legitimate channels and obtain valid visas. In these cases, Muslim governments have made a commitment on behalf of their people to welcome the foreigners as guests and to safeguard their lives and belongings. Finally, the authors argue that the history of conflict among Muslims has weakened the umma.[189]

---

[186] Al-Sayyid, "The Other Face of the Islamist Movement," 16-17.
[187] CIA, *Islamic Activism: A Primer*, 105.
[188] Al-Sayyid, "The Other Face of the Islamist Movement," 18.
[189] Al-Sayyid, "The Other Face of the Islamist Movement," 17.

The book [three] takes a stand against *takfir* (the practice of excommunication), which has been used by factions of the Islamist movements against politicians, intellectuals, non-Muslims, and Muslims who do not interpret their religion "correctly" or who cooperate with non-Muslims. The authors argue that takfir is based on an excessively strict interpretation of Islamic teaching, stemming from a lack of understanding of the true nature of religion, obsession with marginal issues, and the influence of teachers who are not competent scholars of Islam."[190]

In the fourth book the authors continue the theme against an arbitrary imposition of takfir. They "recognize the religious duty of Muslims to call for good and to resist wrong, but they argue that an erroneous interpretation of this duty has prevailed among Islamists.... Militants have also justified the assassination of senior government officials, claiming that these men were no longer Muslims because of their acceptance of secular law.... Finally, the authors advise their followers not to impose their values on those who do not adhere to their interpretations."[191]

Following the decimation of their movement by the Mubarak government of Egypt, aided by al-Jama'a al-Islamiyya's alienation from the population by their vigilante tactics in enforcing their interpretation of individual Muslim conduct, the movement decided to change tactics.

The four texts...constitute a wholesale reversal of the theoretical positions al-Jama'a al-Islamiyya articulated in the late 1970's and early 1980's. This point was reiterated in interviews with the historical leaders that appeared in the Egyptian weekly Al-Mussawar and in the leaders' meetings with members of al-Jama'a al-Islamiyya in several Egyptian prisons. On these occasions the leaders clarified their position on the events of September 11, 2001, in the United States. Karam Zohdi, the leader of al-Jama'a al-Islamiyya in Egypt, and Nageh Ibrahim, the group's theoretician, concurred in saying the attack was incompatible with shari'a, which bans killing civilians of any religion. Ibrahim added that the attacks harmed the Islamist cause by spreading a negative image of Islam and leading to the fall of the Islamist regime in Afghanistan. He also characterized Osama bin Laden as an adventurer with the unrealistic ambition to fight simultaneously the Russians in Chechnya, the Indians in Kashmir, and the United States in Saudi Arabia. According to Nageh Ibrahim, bin Laden engages in Jihad for its own sake; because his goals could be achieved through peaceful methods, armed action is unjustified.[192]

---

[190]Al-Sayyid, "The Other Face of the Islamist Movement," 17.
[191]Al-Sayyid, "The Other Face of the Islamist Movement," 17-18.
[192]Al-Sayyid, "The Other Face of the Islamist Movement," 18.

Following the May 2003 bombings of Western housing areas in Riyadh, Saudi Arabia, Crown Prince Abdullah denounced the actions of the jihadists. Muslim scholars in Saudi Arabia, supposedly following their governments lead, also "condemned" the attacks, but refused to come to grips with the underlying causes.

> A number of Muslim scholars in Saudi Arabia have issued a statement in which they strongly condemned the operation that took place in Riyadh recently. The statement stressed that operations like these violate the Islamic Shari'ah and have nothing to do with the legitimate concept of Jihad. The statement also affirmed that such acts open the door for those who harbor ill intentions toward Islam and want to battle against Muslims. The statement called on Saudi officials to deal with the incident wisely and moderately and to admit that there is a problem that needs to be solved. It also pointed out that dialogue should be encouraged away from security fears...[the Yemen and Egypt model]. The Saudi scholars' statement highlighted the danger of bringing the battle inside the country, warning against exploiting the incident to wage war against curricula, the judiciary system, and the Committee for the Propagation of Virtue and Prevention of Vice. In their statement, the scholars rejected what they called the tyrannical and opportunist stands of the U.S. Administration, highlighting what they described as the growing hatred of the U.S. policies all over the world."[193]

While the scholars want to admit that they have a problem, the problem is obviously not the Saudi system that grows and protects jihadists: They still want to do this. According to the scholars, the Saudis should continue to handle their problems internally, that is, not cooperate in the elimination of Saudi jihadists, and future jihadists, and externally to focus on the "tyrannical and opportunist stands of the U.S. Administration." This is a formula for continued attacks upon the U.S. by Saudi nationals, for future generations.

> A harsher stand, however, was taken in a London-based Arab newspaper.

> On 18 May [2003] the influential *Al-Sharq Al-Awsat* published an editorial calling on Arab societies to confront terrorism. "Silence is not acceptable anymore...the Arab world, with its countries and societies, is facing a dirty war waged by groups that are full of hatred, malice and vindictiveness. Everyone is targeted." Arab societies "should shoulder the full responsibility in confronting this plague and putting an end to it as soon as possible."[194]

---

[193]"Saudi Muslim Figure Cited on Saudi Scholar's Statement Condemning Riyadh Bombing," On Doha Al-Jazirah, Satellite Channel Television, in Arabic, Doha Al-Jazirah, airdate 19 May 2003, GMP20030520000039, 2025 GMT, accessed on Intelink 20 May 2003

[194]"Saudi Arabia: Paper Urged Confrontation of Terrorism," GMP20030518000127, *London Al-Sharq Al Awsat*, 0127 GMT 18 May 2003, accessed on Intelink 20 May 2003.

What is obvious from both the examples of the young jihadists in Yemen, and the al-Jama'a al-Islamiyya, is that the intervention of state power is the prerequisite for "deprogramming" in the first case, and a reevaluation of philosophy and tactics in the second. In both instances the "conversion" came in prison. In the first the concept of the acceptance of the Muslim ruler's right to declare Jihad was emphasized; in the second, the futility of fighting a state power (Egypt) when one can't win. More broadly, the Islamic concept of not fighting a losing Jihad, as in the case of Al-Qa'ida attacking the U.S., India and Russia simultaneously, is the overarching Islamic principle. It is difficult to convince jihadists of the futility of their cause, however, if they are conducting their activities in safe havens, such as Europe.

EUROPE: INCUBATOR OF JIHAD

The modern Jihad would not be possible without the European environment that provides for a "rear" safe haven and logistics base. Jihadists have been contained by oppressive governments in the Arab world. However, the method of containment, a combination of force and focusing the jihadists outward (supporting Jihad and proselytizing) have forced them into Europe and the Muslim periphery (Africa, Asia, and to some extent Latin America) where Jihad has taken root and thrived. European societies and governments, especially, are ill-prepared to cope with jihadist activities. This is especially ironic given the long history of European Christian-Arab/Turkic Muslim conflict. The U.S. is almost equally ill-prepared to deal with the jihadist phenomenon within its borders, but a realization of the threat and strengthening of laws have at least positioned the U.S. to respond. The Europeans are closer to the threat, have a larger proportional problem than does the U.S., and are (deliberately) slow to identify the problem. All Arab regimes consider unmonitored and uncontrolled Islamic institutions, Mosques, and imams, a threat. These Muslim regimes know what they are dealing with. This type of governmental "oversight" of religious institutions is anathema to both U.S., and especially, European societies. This has opened wide the door for jihadists to continue their activities, and to strengthen their ranks in Europe.

Bernard Lewis describes the Saudi-funded spreading of the Wahabbi message of Jihad:

> In modern usage the word madrasa [traditionally a center of higher education, scholarship, teaching, and research] has acquired a negative meaning; it has come to denote a center for indoctrination in bigotry and violence. A revealing example may be seen in the backgrounds of a number of Turks arrested on suspicion of complicity in terrorist activities. Every single one of them was born and educated in Germany, not one in Turkey. The German government does not supervise the religious education of minority groups. The Turkish government keeps a watchful eye on these matters. In Europe and America, because of the reluctance of the state to involve itself in religious matters, the teaching of Islam in schools and elsewhere has in general been totally unsupervised by authority. This situation clearly favors those with the fewest scruples, the strongest convictions, and the most money.[195]

Almost by definition, a jihadist, dedicated to the overthrow of their home government and the implementation of shar'ia, will be "persecuted" in their home state for their "religious beliefs." This almost guarantees them asylum status in most of Europe. Should they actually be convicted of jihadist activities, usually crimes to include murder, in their home state, European nations will usually not honor an extradition request (including to the U.S.) if the jihadist is subject to the death penalty, as is the case of most hard-core jihadists. These jihadists, dedicated to their cause, continue their Jihad

---

[195]Lewis, *The Crisis of Islam*, 128-129.

in Europe by preaching, fund raising, and recruiting. The base of their activity is the Mosque. Until recently, because of Western sensitivities to a certain perception of the inviolability of a house of worship, this approach has allowed for the creation of "citadels of Jihad" throughout Europe.

The jihadist pattern of highlighting the centrality of the Mosque as a European "castle" has an interesting parallel in Islamic history.

> During his interminable journeys, Hasan was not only occupied with winning converts to the cause. He was also concerned with finding a new kind of base — not a clandestine tryst in a city, in constant danger of discovery and disruption, but a remote and inaccessible stronghold, from which he could with impunity direct his war against the Seljuk Empire. His choice finally fell on the castle of Alamut, built on a narrow ridge on the top of a high rock in the heart of the Elburz mountains....The seizure of Alamut was carefully prepared.... Some of the people in Alamut were converted.... With his followers now installed in the castle, Hasan left...for the neighborhood of Alamut, where he stayed for some time in concealment. Then, on Wednesday, 4 September 1090, he was brought secretly into the castle in disguise, but in due course his identity became known. The former owner realized what had happened, but could do nothing to stop or change it.[196]

Ismaeli successors to Hasan followed this same pattern to acquire more castles and propagate their beliefs. Modern jihadists follow this pattern in Europe, and elsewhere, to establish their "remote and inaccessible stronghold" that is not in "constant danger of discovery and disruption" (as they would be in Arab countries), "from which he [they] could with impunity direct his [their] war [Jihad] against" their home countries, and now, the United States.

Central to this Western vulnerability is a conception that there is a parallel between a Church, a Mosque and a Synagogue. This basic misperception has created the jihadist "castles" in Europe that are now just being discovered.

> The new community [Islam] was to have no priesthood, no hierarchy, no central see. Its mosque was its public forum and military drill ground as well as its place of common worship.[197]

> For three centuries, Christianity was a persecuted religion — different from, sometimes opposed to, and often oppressed by the state authority. In the course of their long struggle, Christians developed a distinctive institution — the church, with its own laws and courts, its own hierarchy and chain of authority. Christians sometimes speak of "The Synagogue" and "The Mosque" to denote the religious institutions of the Jewish and Muslim faiths.

---

[196]Lewis, *The Assassins: A Radical Sect in Islam*, 42-43.

[197] Hitti, *History of the Arabs: From the Earliest Times to the Present*, 121.

But these are inappropriate terms, the projection of Christian notions on non-Christian religions. For the Jew or the Muslim, the synagogue or the mosque is a building, a place of worship and study, no more. Until modern times and the spread of Christian norms and influence, neither had ever had, for its own worshipers, the institutional sense of the Christian term.[198]

The mosques of Europe also perform a function that has not been available to Islam (outside the hajj) since its earliest years. Muslims coming from many countries pray in their local European mosques. There are even instances when Shi'as and Sunnis pray in the same mosques. This has allowed, as did the anti-Soviet Jihad in Afghanistan, for an internationalization of the Jihad. Jihadists, through mosques in Europe, have connected with each other throughout the Muslim world. A similar and deadly phenomenon occurred in December 1992 when Israel expelled 415 Sunni Palestinians (mostly Hamas members) to southern Lebanon, where they were welcomed by Hizballah (Shi'as). They were trained in bomb making and introduced to the virtues of suicide bombings. Israel has suffered from this unforeseen consequence since.

The total number of mosques in Europe is unknown. It is difficult to make an accurate count because Western governments are loathe to keep these types of statistics on "religious" facilities, and the size of mosques can vary from large, stand-alone buildings to apartments.[199] The threat posed by mosques is just beginning to be realized.

The number of Muslims in Europe is likewise unknown. In addition, some countries have statistics on numbers of converts to Islam, as well as citizen status of Muslims, while others do not. An estimate for 2003 was that about 6 million Muslims lived in France, 3 million in Germany, 1.5 million in the UK, and 1.4 million in Italy.[200]

The vast majority of Muslims are drawn to Europe for economic reasons. However, a significant jihadist presence is drawn by the highly permissive operational environment, especially as compared to their home countries. Once in Europe, jihadists naturally interact with their Muslim coreligionists, and often feel compelled by their faith to preach Jihad. For visa/asylum purposes, and according to their faith which allows multiple wives, they marry local Muslim, or native, women (usually with resident status). Their children often attain the citizenship of their European host nation at birth. This process deeply embeds the jihadist in Europe.

A December 2002 poll taken by the British Broadcasting Company (BBC) among the Muslim population may shed some light on the potential magnitude of the problem.[201] Given the poll results, and a Muslim population in Great Britain of 1.5 million, the abso-

---

[198]Lewis, What Went Wrong, 97-98.

[199]Muslims in Europe: The Mosques," Saudi Aramco World 30, no. 1 (January/February 1979).

[200]"European Muslim Population," Muslim Population Worldwide, URL: *http://www.islamicpopulation.com/europe_islam.html*, accessed January 2004.

[201]"Muslims Poll," ICM Polls for BBC Radio, December 2002, URL: *http://www.icmresearch.co.uk/reviews/2002/bbc-today-muslims-dec-02.htm*, accessed January 2004.

lute number of the respondents who hold anti-Western views, and who exhibit a willingness to harm Britain, or support those who do, can be derived as follows:

Britain is waging a war against Islam (70%=1.05 million);
Al-Qa'ida not to blame for 9/11 (50%=.75 million);
Further Al-Qa'ida attacks on the U.S. would be justified (11%=16.5 thousand);
Al-Qa'ida attacks on Britain would be justified (8%=12 thousand);
Feel patriotic about Britain (67%=1.005 million)-[therefore its reciprocal:
Don't feel patriotic about Britain-(33%=495 thousand)].

Based on this poll, Britain may have 12 thousand Muslims from which to draw jihadists for an attack, and a potential 495 thousand Muslims who may be willing in some way to support them.

The problem is large and getting worse, as Muslims living in non-Muslim countries in Europe come to grips with a resurgent and activist Islam. This may be especially acute among converts, and second-generation Muslims in Europe who are attempting to find their Islamic identity, and are being introduced to the fundamental Islamic concepts of the spreading of the faith, and of Jihad as a method of doing so. Jihadist recruiters are well aware of the vulnerability to persuasion of both converts and second-generation Muslims. The West's general inclination not to question the teachings of a religious leader has also led to the appointment of official chaplains at prisons that spread jihadist interpretations of Islam.

From a European/Western perspective the problem of Islamic radicalism is viewed as one of assimilation. To the degree that Muslims assimilate into the greater society, they will become less "radical." However, the real question is: Can a devout Muslim live in a non-Muslim country? This is especially important in view of the global trend toward a greater devoutness within Islam. If not, is assimilation into European society even possible, and if they can't assimilate, will they leave or become radicalized?

Muslim law and tradition devote much attention to the legal situation of the non-Muslim under Muslim rule, which is discussed at great length and regulated in great detail. Very little, however, is said about the corresponding problem of the Muslim under non-Muslim rule. This is not surprising. During the early centuries of Islamic history, when Muslim traditions were collected and committed to writing and the basic rules of Muslim jurisprudence were laid down, the Muslim state and community were expanding almost continuously, and great numbers of non-Muslims were brought under Muslim rule. In contrast, virtually no Muslim territories were lost to non-Muslim invaders, and apart from occasional tactical withdrawals along the Byzantine frontier, usually of limited extent and brief duration, the loss of Muslim territory was for several centuries unknown and therefore inconceivable. It was not until the eleventh century that the reconquest in Europe, the irruptions of the Christian peoples of the Caucasus into the Middle East, and the invasions of the

Crusaders and, later, of the heathen Mongols, created an entirely new situation. But by then the basic norms of the shari'a had long since been established.[202]

The initial assumption of the jurists in discussing this matter is clearly that for a Muslim to live under non-Muslim rule is undesirable, and, according to some, forbidden, and only dire necessity could lead a Muslim to do such a thing. Until modern times, the entire discussion of the position of the Muslim under non-Muslim rule was considered in relation to two situations-the practical needs of the short-term or long-term visitor to an infidel land, and the sad predicament of a Muslim community conquered by infidel invaders. What never seems to have occurred to any of the classical jurists was that great numbers of Muslims, of their own free will, would go and live under the rule of non-Muslim governments, subject themselves and their families to non-Muslim personal law, and send their children to be educated in non-Muslim schools. But this is precisely what has happened. This is the situation in which many millions of Muslims from North Africa, the Middle East, South and Southeast Asia, and elsewhere now find themselves in every country in western Europe....It is clear that many of them still feel that it is their God-given duty to command what is good and forbid what is evil, in their new no less than their old homes.[203]

This Islamic jurisprudence presents the devout Muslim with a dilemma. First-generation immigrants to Europe and the U.S. already have made a determination that economic/political factors outweigh their religious concerns. Their offspring and converts did not make that determination and are therefore more likely to have to weigh their religious convictions with their national allegiance. Both groups are thus more susceptible to arguments that their religious obligations outweigh their allegiance to a non-Muslim government. Second-generation Muslim immigrants, seeking to reaffirm their Islamic credentials, and willing to challenge their parents, are more likely to be radicalized than their parents who appreciate the opportunities offered by the non-Muslim country to which they chose to immigrate. An incident that illustrates this point was a CBS TV network "60 Minutes" interview done with American students at an Islamic school in Brooklyn, NY, shortly after the World Trade Center attacks. A group of pre-teen or young teenage girls from the school, appearing in mannerism and speech to be at least second-generation residents of the U.S., but dressed in Muslim attire, was interviewed. Although condemning the destruction of the Twin Towers, they stated that an attack on the "navy yard" would be a legitimate target. In a highly unusual concession, the following week these girls again appeared on "60 Minutes" where the interviewer explained that the girls' parents insisted that the girls "clarify" their remarks. The "clarification" was that the "navy yard" that the girls meant was a legitimate target was the "Haifa Navy Yard." It is doubtful that these girls from Brooklyn knew anything about

---

[202]Lewis, *Islam and the West*, 40-41.
[203]Lewis, *Islam and the West*, 41.

the Israeli naval facilities in Haifa, but, were well aware of the "Brooklyn Navy Yard" located not far from their homes.

Local converts also have the dilemma of allegiance to their native countries, or to their new religion. Like most converts, they tend to be more zealous in their religious practices. In essence, they must prove to themselves and others that they are "good Muslims." It would not be unnatural for these people, who have "left their native culture" (Islam is a complete way of life), and who have embraced Islam, to now want to live under shari'a. Still not divorced from the democratic values in which they were raised, they may even consider it their "right" as a European or American exercising "religious freedom" to live within their home countries under shari'a.

The jurisprudence on the issue of Muslims living in non-Muslim countries has not been settled. This leaves room for modern jihadists to exploit the issue. An article in a Saudi-owned London paper that takes issue with a recent fatwa on this subject issued by Al-Azhar in Cairo is illustrative of this point.

> Al-Azhar has issued a strange fatwa saying that it is impermissible under the shari'ah to acquire American citizenship. The fatwa justifies this by saying "carrying the citizenship of a country is tantamount to a contract of allegiance to the country." The strange fatwa adds, "It is impermissible to acquire the citizenship of a non-Muslim country involved in a war with a Muslim country. In time of peace, a Muslim can carry the citizenship of that country."...An American Muslim reading such fatwas would face one of two alternatives: either to reject it or act by it. If he rejects it, he would be accused of committing a sin for not obeying a religious institution like Al-Azhar. If he agreed to act by this fatwa, it would turn his life into hell.... What happens to the millions of Palestinians who hold Israeli citizenship and constitute a real force inside Israeli society? What service will this fatwa render to Zionism if these Palestinians gave up their citizenship, lost their homes, and went to live in the West Bank and Gaza strip, particularly when Israel is in a state of war with the Muslims? What happens to the millions of Muslims in Britain, which is joining the United States in the war against Iraq? What happens to millions of Muslims in Spain, Australia, and Canada — countries that are joining the United States in its military effort? If Al-Azhar issues such unconsidered fatwas, what can we say to hundreds of unlearned and quasi-jurisprudents who issue fatwas every day on everything? What will the position of the Muslim young people be as they listen to these people issuing controversial fatwas on everything without knowledge or responsibility?[204]

> When the question [Muslims living under non-Muslim rule] is discussed at all it is, naturally enough, under the same general heading, Jihad, and in the same

---

[204]"Writer Criticizes Al-Azhar's 'Strange' Fatwa on Acquiring Foreign Citizenship," *London Al-Sharq al-Awsa*t, in Arabic, 17 March 2003, URL: <https://datawarehouse10.dia.ic.gov/cgi-bin/webisprt?000009ce+M4+repbrag>, accessed 18 March 2003, 3.

categories, permanent resident and temporary visitor, as is the status of non-Muslim under Muslim rule. In the earliest juristic literature, the position of a Muslim permanently resident in a non-Muslim land is considered only in one contingency, that of an infidel in the land of the infidels who sees the light and embraces Islam....The question they discuss is whether he may remain where he is or must leave his home and migrate to a Muslim country. The Shi'a jurists, more attuned to the idea of surviving in a hostile environment and under a hostile authority, allow him to stay and indeed see him as an outpost and beacon of Islam. The majority of Sunni jurists, accustomed to the association of religion and authority, insist that he must leave and remove himself to a Muslim land where he can live in accordance with the holy law of Islam. In this he would be following the sacred precedent set by the Prophet and his Companions when they left their homes in pagan Mecca and undertook the migration (hijira) to Medina, where they established the first Muslim state and community. Some jurists even go so far as to say that if he remains where he is and his country is subsequently conquered by the Muslims, then his non-Muslim family and his property are liable to be treated as booty by the conquerors in the same way as those of his infidel neighbors and compatriots.[205]

The question of a Muslim traveler to the lands of the infidels for a voluntary or involuntary, brief or protracted visit was of more practical concern and receives more attention. Prisoners, captured in war or at sea, had no choice, and the jurists offer guidelines on how a Muslim who suffers this misfortune should conduct himself until he is ransomed or exchanged or escapes. As regards voluntary visitors, the first question to be decided was whether such visits are permissible at all in law and, if so, under what circumstances and subject to what rules. Malik, the founder of the Malaki school, allows Muslims to visit the lands of the infidels for one purpose only — to ransom captives. It is significant that almost all the reports of the Moroccan ambassadors to the various courts of Europe are headed "Report of a Mission for the Ransoming of Captives" — no doubt in order to avoid possible legal difficulties for themselves or their sovereign.[206]

Malaki jurists continued to argue the issue of traveling to the land of the infidel. The most lenient opinion allows: "...a general tolerance to Muslim travel and temporary residence abroad and allow a Muslim to accept aman [safe conduct/visa] from a non-Muslim government and stay for a while in a non-Muslim country.... The acceptance by a Muslim of a non-Muslim aman is subject to certain conditions from the Muslim side, the most important of which is that he be able to "manifest the signs of Islam."[207]

---

[205]Lewis, *Islam and the West*, 48-49.
[206]Lewis, *Islam and the West*, 49.
[207]Lewis, *Islam and the West*, 49-50.

But the practice of Islam means more than worship, important as that may be. It means a whole way of life, prescribed in detail by the holy texts and treatises based on them. Nor is that all. The primary duty of the Muslim as set forth not once, but many times in the Qur'an is "to command good and forbid evil." It is not enough to do good and refrain from evil as a personal choice. It is incumbent upon Muslims also to command and forbid — that is, to exercise authority. The same principle applied in general to the holy law, which be not only obeyed but also enforced.... For this reason, in any encounter between Islam and unbelief, Islam must dominate. That is why mosques must overtop non-Muslim places of worship and never be overtopped by them [thus Al-Aqsa mosque on Temple Mount in Jerusalem, topping the Church of the Holy Sepulcher], and why — on this point the jurists are unanimous — a Muslim man may marry a non-Muslim women, but a non-Muslim man may not, on pain of death, marry a Muslim women. In marriage, so the jurists believed, the husband is always the dominant partner."[208]

The question of "permanent residence" in a non-Muslim country became acute, not because of immigration, a modern phenomenon, but because of Christian reconquest.

The problem, as usually formulated in the judicial literature, is as follows: "If their country has been conquered by the Christians, may Muslims stay or must they migrate to a Muslim land?".... In a characteristic and frequently cited saying, the Prophet denounces and rejects any Muslim who chooses to live among the polytheists.... In the early centuries of Islam the question of hijra [migration] was purely theoretical and some jurists, notably of the Hanafi school, argued that the obligation of hijra ceased to operate after the Muslim conquest of Mecca...The tide of Christian reconquest gave the question a new relevance and urgency, and the Maliki jurists of the West, confronted by the subjugation of extensive Muslim territories in Sicily, Spain, and Portugal, gave a different answer. The obligation of hijra, they declared, had not lapsed but will remain in effect until the Day of Judgment. The only questions are when and in what circumstances it applies and when and for whom it may be remitted.[209]

Religious tolerance in the West allows for a more lenient interpretation favoring a Muslim's being allowed to stay in a non-Muslim country following a reconquest. What is left unanswered is a problem that Muslim jurists did not face: large numbers of Muslims voluntarily immigrating to non-Muslim countries. There are, however, rules of conduct and circumstances that can be applied in either instance.

Some jurists find authority in the Qur'an and hadiths for exemption on the ground of physical or financial incapacity; some invoke the principle of

---

[208]Lewis, *Islam and the West,* 52-53.
[209]Lewis, *Islam and the West,* 51-52.

darura, necessity, both personal and communal, to allow significant post-ponements of the inevitable departure; and some allow Muslims to stay, in the hope of "guiding the people of unbelief to the truth and saving them from error." But all agree that it is a bad thing for Muslims to remain under non-Muslim rule, the principal disagreement being whether such as [sic] action falls under the heading of disapproved or forbidden — or, to put it the other way around, whether emigration is commanded or merely recommended. The key question is whether they are permitted to practice their religion or, more precisely, to "manifest the signs of Islam." If they are not, then all agree that they must leave. If they are, then the moderates see their continued presence as disapproved, and the more rigorous jurists insist that even then they are bound by religious law to leave. The Moroccan jurist Ahmad al-Wansharisi, writing in the final stages of the Christian reconquest of Spain, insists that even if the Christian conquerors are both just and tolerant, the Muslims are still required to leave — indeed, even more so, since under such a regime the danger of apostasy would be correspondingly greater.[210]

It is the duty of a Muslim, wherever he may be, to bring faith to the unbelievers. Islam, unlike Christianity, has no professional missionaries but assigns this task to all Muslims alike. It is, however, strictly forbidden for a dhimmi to try to convert a Muslim to his religion, and if by any mischance he succeeds, the penalty for apostasy is death. From a Muslim religious point of view, this discrepancy is both logical and proper. To promote the true faith is a divine commandment. To abandon it, or to persuade another to do so, is both a mortal sin and a capital crime. There are some who followed this argument to its logical conclusion and maintained that authentic Muslim life is possible only under a Muslim government. There are others who reject this extremist view and admit the possibility of living a Muslim life under a non-Muslim government, provided that the government meets certain specific requirements. The Hanafi school, in this as in most other matters inclined toward moderate positions, was satisfied with basic tolerance, and imposed migration only when Muslims suffered forced conversion or were prevented from performing their religious duties. Even then, emigration was obligatory only for those who had the necessary means. The Malaki school, as well as other eastern schools, was more rigorous and regarded emigration as being at the very least recommended and in most cases obligatory....For the most rigorous, even in the most favorable circumstances, Muslims are forbidden to stay and are required to leave."[211]

The problem faced by the Muslim immigrant in Europe is an inability to practice all aspects of his religion.

---

[210]Lewis, *Islam and the West*, 52.

[211] Lewis, *Islam and the West*, 53.

The resulting dilemma is epitomized in the no-doubt apocryphal complaint of a recent Muslim immigrant to Europe: "We allowed Christians to practice and even enforce monogamy under Muslim rule, so why shouldn't you allow us to practice polygamy under Christian rule?" The difficulty arises not only from conflicting social mores, as in this and similar cases, but also — more especially — from an understanding of identity and jurisdiction that is clearly out of accord with the accepted practice of most of the modern world, including some of the Muslim states. In Turkey, shari'a law has been legally abolished but was for long in fact unofficially maintained in remote rural areas. As a result, many children born of polygamous "marriages" were legitimate under shari'a law but illegitimate under state law. What the jurists principally fear when Muslims live under non-Muslim law is the reverse — a disastrous process that could destroy the very fabric of the Muslim family and therefore Muslim society."[212]

What jihadists fear is Western social values and laws that detract from the primacy of the Muslim male. It is not, therefore, unusual to find jihadists resident in Europe who have additional wives elsewhere in the Muslim world. It is doubtful that European governments check for this polygamy before granting asylum and citizenship based upon a "marriage" to a European national.

What then happens to the modern jihadist, and his family, living in Europe, or elsewhere in the West? Not only is he not under shari'a, but he is engulfed in a permissive culture that is totally alien to Islam. He cannot, however, conduct Jihad if he settles in a Muslim country for fear of arrest and deportation to his home country. He may or may not be in his host country legally, and considering himself a jihadist, likely does not feel constrained by Muslim law not to act against his refuge country. In fact, he may feel obligated to do so.

If the Muslim entered the dar al-Harb without aman, he has no obligation to observe its laws and regulations as those under aman. In Muslim legal theory, the Muslim in a non-Muslim territory without aman is at war with that territory. He is, therefore, under no obligation to submit to the law of non-Muslim territories, although in the meantime he is not expected to engage in hostile actions. If the Muslim, however, enters dar al-Harb by permission of the iman [jihadists would consider this to be the case] he may seize property or take prisoners of war in the same way as the jihadists are permitted during actual fighting.[213]

Another phenomenon that has reemerged in the modern era is that of Muslim prisoners being forcibly taken to non-Muslim countries. It is implied that they must seek to return to a Muslim country, but must still abide by laws of Jihad.

---

[212]Lewis, *Islam and the West*, 55.
[213]Khadduri, *War and Peace in the Law of Islam,* 173.

Muslim warriors who fall into the hands of the enemy and are taken to dar al-Harb are under obligation to live up to their promises if they are set free on parole.... If, on the other hand, the prisoners gave no promises, they were not only free to flee but also to destroy enemy property or kill non-Muslims on their way back to dar al-Islam.[214]

European integration and the concurrent liberalization of laws governing individual rights came at a very opportune time for jihadists. Conservative elements within European governments that would favor tougher laws governing the conduct of their governments toward jihadists find themselves stymied as their country's laws were trumped by overall European Union liberal concepts of individual rights. The European Union requirement for the elimination of the death penalty (and non-extradition to countries that would subject someone to it), and the open borders within Europe, allow Europe to become the safe haven for Jihad. A European fallacy, developed to both deal with European terrorist groups of the 1970s-1980s and to placate Arab governments, of imputing a duality to terrorist organizations — the concept of political and military "wings" — makes it easier for jihadists to operate. There is no distinction in Jihad between a "political" and "military" wing. An individual's actions at any given time may be one or the other, but Jihad is ultimately a religious-military endeavor. Anti-terrorist laws, by their very nature, apply only to named "terrorist" groups. Groups that qualify as "terrorist" vary between European countries, and between Europe and the United States. Seeking to prosecute individuals, law enforcement — to comply with the laws — must establish a "link" between an individual and a "terrorist" group. European jihadists, although often associated with Middle East jihadist groups, are united in their support for Jihad, not by membership in a "terrorist" organization. Therefore, when prosecuted, European jihadists rightly deny membership in a "terrorist" group. They are not terrorists, but, jihadists, which is not in and of itself illegal.

European laws, generally structured to combat terrorism of the 1970s and 1980s, are ill-prepared to counter Jihad. Jihad is not an action; it is a belief that leads to various actions. Some of those actions can fit under the category of terrorism, others, however, are more akin to freedom of speech, religion, and assembly. There are laws against incitement to race hatred, which are often applicable, but not often used. Other laws prohibit support to a terrorist organization, but Jihad is not a terrorist organization, although groups such as Al-Qa'ida do commit terrorist acts. Prosecuting the perpetrators of terrorist acts after the fact does not get at the root of the problem. The greatest difficulty in prosecuting many of these cases is that often they are based solely upon the fruits of intelligence collection. This makes the provision of proof difficult, under the constraint of not compromising intelligence sources and methods. Examples of European (and Canadian) laws that are ill-equipped to contain jihadist activity abound.

An examining magistrate of the Federal Supreme Court has rejected an arrest warrant for the German Islamist Christian Ganczarski, who is hiding in Saudi

[214]Khadduri, *War and Peace in the Law of Islam*, 173.

Arabia. Ganczarski, a suspected member of the Al-Qa'ida terror group, is considered a close aide of the Djerba attacker Nikzar Nawar, who blew up a truck filled with gas in front of a synagogue [in Tunisia] in April 2002. A total of 21 tourists, including 14 Germans were killed.... [T]he examining magistrate saw no "conclusive evidence" concerning Ganczarski's knowledge of the planned attack when he examined the arrest warrant... Ganczarski, who lived in Duisberg at the time, received a telephone call from Nawar approximately two hours before the attack. In the telephone call, taped by the security authorities, Nawar asked his friend to bless him."[215]

Treating this incident as an individual criminal act, as opposed to trying Ganczarski as a jihadist, makes the case all but impossible. Had Nawar and Ganczarski been Nazis, the German legal system may be better prepared to handle them.

An absurdity of European law is the case of Mullah Krekar, the head of the jihadist group Ansar al-Islam in Kurdish Iraq. Krekar was granted refugee "protection" in Norway in 1991, because his life was in danger. He now claims, paradoxically, that the notoriety received by Ansar al-Islam, and the disclosure that he is its leader, now make his life even more in danger. It is an argument that seems to play well in Europe. He was arrested in the Netherlands, based on a Jordanian request, but was not extradited to Jordan. Instead he was extradited to Norway when Dutch authorities believed that he may be let go because, according to the Netherlands Justice Minister Donner "Jordan had not answered questions."[216] Unni Fries, legal council for the PST [Norwegian] anti-terrorism police, is investigating whether Krekar "committed acts considered criminal under Norwegian law. If he allows us, we will question him in days to come." Under Norwegian law, she stressed, he would not be interrogated against his will,[217] nor, it might be added, incarcerated "against his will." Mullah Krekar is now suing the Norwegian government for his "illegal" detention.

Canadian laws also seem to have a problem in dealing with jihadists.

A Federal Court judge said yesterday he is disturbed by the government's treatment of a suspected member of Usama Bin Ladin's terrorist network who has spent nearly two years in jail without being charged with a crime — going so far as to compare Mahmoud Jaballah to a prisoner at Guantanamo Bay.... "Mr. Jaballah, I'm sorry it's been such a long process for you and your family," the

---

[215]"No Arrest Warrant Against German Islamist," Munich Focus Online, in German, online ed., 9 May 2003, URL: <https://datawarehouse10.dia.ic.gov/fcgi-bin/webisdoc?DOC72D+59061+00000b02+repbrag>, accessed 12 May 2003.

[216]"Kurd Mullah Krekar Expelled," Rotterdam NRC Handelsblad, online ed., in Dutch, 14 January 2003, URL: <https://datawarehouse10.dia.ic.gov/cgi-bin/webisprt?00000ab2+M4+dibrarb>, accessed 14 January 2003.

[217]"Norwegian Police Want to Question Iraqi Kurd Suspect," Paris AFP North European Service, online ed., in English, 14 Jan 2003, URL: <https://datawarehouse10.dia.ic.gov/cgi-bin/webisprt?00000a36+M4+dibrarb>, accessed 15 January 2003.

judge added.... Mr. Jaballah, a Scarborough Islamic school principal whom the Canadian Security Intelligence Service (CSIS) has linked to [Egyptian] Al-Jihad, a terrorist group tied to Al-Qa'ida.... Mr. Jaballah, an Egyptian who came to Canada in 1996 using a false passport, has reportedly met with Ayman Al Zawahiri, Bin Ladin's second-in-command....Mr. Jaballah was first arrested in March 1999, after the federal government issued a national security certificate under section 40.1 of the then-Immigration act, which, if rubber-stamped by a judge, paves the way for deportation proceedings to begin. A federal Court judge later quashed the certificate, saying he believed Mr. Jaballah was not a threat to national security.... In August 2001, after re-examining the evidence — which remains secret for security reasons — authorities convinced...the minister of citizenship and immigration, and...the solicitor-general...to issue a second national security certificate. In the summer of 2002, while [the evidence against Mr. Jaballah was still being considered by the courts] the government unveiled the New Immigration and Refugee Protection Act, which forces authorities to determine whether deportees will face violent persecution upon returning to their home countries.... In August 2002, officials working for the Immigration Minister concluded Mr. Jaballah would likely be killed or tortured if he is sent back to Egypt. Now, in order for the section 40.1 hearing to resume [the Immigration Minister and], the Solicitor General, have to decide whether Mr. Jaballah should still be deported in light of the apparent threat to his safety. The court has been waiting for that decision for the past eight months. "Do you know of any other claim to authority in this country where a minister can hold someone in solitary confinement for that time?" [The] judge asked lawyers for both sides....[A] lawyer representing Citizenship and Immigration, said the government needs more time, adding "national security is so unlike the criminal process".... The immigration and Refugee Board yesterday rejected his claim for refugee status, ruling there are "serious reasons" to believe he is linked to terrorist organizations. But the board said Mr. Jaballah's wife and their four children, who were born outside Canada, should be allowed to stay here.[218]

Australia also has a legal problem in dealing in jihadists.

Australian taxi driver and Muslim convert Jack "Jihad" Thomas will not be charged under Australian law when he is finally deported from Pakistan, his lawyer said Tuesday.... Although the Pakistani government initially claimed he was a trained terrorist with links to Al-Qa'ida, interior ministry officials revealed last month that they had nothing to charge him with.[219]

---

[218]Michael Friscolanti, "Judge Sorry for Delay in Terror Suspect's Case; Held 20 Months: Compares refugee to Prisoners at Guantanamo Bay," *Toronto National Post*, online ed., 12 April 2003, URL: <*https://datawarehouse10.dia.ic.gov/cgi-bin/ webisprt?00000a72+M4+repbrag*>, accessed 17 April 2003.

There are, however, some creative applications of laws being employed to thwart jihadists in Europe.

> The Central Muslim Spiritual Board of Russia (TsDUM) may be liquidated as a religious organization if it ignores the prosecutor's warning it has received, the Russian Prosecutor General's Office has said. The federal law On Countering Extremist Activity stipulates that if "violations that served as grounds for a warning are not eliminated within 13 months from the issuance of the warning, and, moreover, if new facts indicating extremism in the activity of this organization are discovered, the public or religious organization can be liquidated....The prosecutor regard[s] TsDUM's statement on declaring a Jihad on the U.S. over the war in Iraq...made at a rally in Ufa on April 3, as a sign of extremism, particularly the fueling of inter-religious discord."[220]

The British have also been very pro-active in attempting to eliminate jihadist activities.

> A fanatical Muslim cleric who urged his followers to murder Americans, Hindus and Jews was jailed for nine years yesterday. Abdullah el-Faisal was told that he had "fanned the flames of hostility" with his racist sermons and should serve at least half his sentence before being deported. El-Faisal, 39, was found guilty last month of three charges of soliciting murder and three counts of stirring up racial hatred. He toured Britain for four years urging audiences to follow the teachings of Usama bin Ladin and kill "unbelievers" as part of the Jihad, or holy war.... The prosecution for soliciting murder, which has a maximum sentence of life, was the first in more than 100 years under the 1861 Offences Against the Person Act.[221]

> British Home Office Secretary David Blunkett announced yesterday that Britain revoked the British citizenship of Egyptian fundamentalist Abu-Hamzah [Al-Masri], who had praised the attacks of 11 September 2001. The British authorities earlier banned him from delivering sermons at the (Finsbery Park) mosque in northern London.... Speaking on BBC radio, Blunkett said: "I sent him a letter on revoking his citizenship." Al-Masri now faces the prospect of deportation to his home country. Blunkett pointed out: "The problem lies not in what Al-Masri says, but in the encouragement of people to take part in Jihad. They encourage people to fight us abroad." However, Blunkett denied

---

[219]"Australian Terror Suspect No Longer Facing Charges," Hong Kong AFP, in English, 03 June 2003, URL: <*https://datawarehouse10.dia.ic.gov/fcgi-bin/webisdoc?DOC72D+303459+00000b72 +repbrag*>, accessed 03 June 2003.

[220]"Russian Prosecutors Say Muslim Council May Be Disbanded for Jihad Against U.S.," *Moscow Interfax*, online ed., in English, CEP20030404000119 0947 GMT, 4 April 2003, accessed on Intelink 4 April 2003.

[221]Steve Bird, "Muslim Cleric is Jailed for Urging Followers to Kill," *The Times London*, online ed., in English, 8 Mar 2003, URL: <*https://datawarehouse10.dia.ic.gov/cgi-bin/webisprt? 0000098e+M4+repbrag*>, accessed 10 March 2003.

that this step signals the beginning of moves to pursue dual-citizenship people. Also, he said that no one will be sent to his country if he will face a death penalty there.... The radio [BBC] said that Egyptian fundamentalist Abu-Hamzah is the first person against whom rules, which call for revoking the British citizenship of dual-nationality persons who are believed to be working against the country's vital interests, are applied.[222]

Some countries, including the Netherlands, are invoking laws more applicable to the Second World War in an attempt to prosecute jihadist teachings.

The trial of 12 suspected Muslim extremists charged with aiding Usama Bin Ladin's network by recruiting combatants for the Islamic Jihad, or holy war, opened on Monday 12 May in Rotterdam. The men are facing charges that range from forgery and drug trafficking to "aiding the enemy of the Dutch state and her allies in a time of armed conflict. The enemy in this case is the Afghan Taliban regime and the network," [a member] of the Dutch national prosecutor's office told AFP.[223]

Modifications in Netherlands legislation are due so as to improve the fight against terrorism, Joan de Wijkerslooth, chairman of the Council of Prosecutors General, said last week during the presentation of the Public Prosecution Office's annual report. "Can we actually accept that recruiting Jihad activists is not regarded as a criminal offense in the Netherlands?" he wondered.... The problem we have to cope with in this regard is that we may well be able to call Al-Qa'ida a proscribed organization, but that it is not the kind of organization with a membership structure as stipulated by law. We are working with concepts that belong to tennis clubs. We know their membership list and if these people start committing criminal offenses, the organization can be proscribed. A terrorist organization, however, has an entirely different mode of operation. If such an organization is banned today, a new organization will be created the next day.[224]

A non-European country that appears to have adequately adapted its laws to counter a nascent jihadist threat is Mauritania.

---

[222]"London-Based Egyptian Fundamentalist Views Revocation of UK Citizenship," *London Al-Sharq al-Awsat,* online ed., 6 April 2003, URL: <*https://datawarehouse10.dia.ic.gov/cgi-bin/webisprt?00000a4a+M4+repbrag*>, accessed 7 April 2003.

[223]"Trial of 12 'Suspected Muslim Extremists' Opens in Rotterdam 12 May," *Paris AFP North European Service,* online ed., in English, 12 May 2003, URL: <*https://datawarehouse10.dia.ic.gov/fcgi-bin/webisdoc?DOC72D+76795+00000b02+repbrag*>, accessed on Intelink 12 May 2003.

[224]"Netherlands Prosecutor Urges Legal Changes to Improve Fight Against Terrorism," *Rotterdam NRC Handelsblad,* online ed., in Dutch, 19 May 2003, URL: <*https://datawarehouse10.dia.ic.gov/fcgi-bin/webisdoc?DOC72D+169663+00000b32+repbrag*>, accessed on Intelink 21 May 2003, 3.

Thirty-six people were charged Tuesday 3 June [2003] with "plotting against the constitutional order".... The suspects, arrested in early May, were also charged with incitement to damage security at home and abroad and of belonging to illegal organizations.... Last month, Mauritanian Prime Minister Cheikh El-Avia Ould Mohamed Khouna warned of the dangers posed by Islamic extremists and against youngsters being drawn to their cause. A number of Islamic activists, including some imams and religious leaders, were arrested and accused of "recruitment" and "subversive scheming." The prime minister said extremists hoped to use Mauritania as a new base, after being harassed out of other countries. "They have profited from the spirit of openness and tolerance which our people display."[225]

It seems that propagating beliefs that require adherence to shari'a, by definition, are unconstitutional, since they deny the very validity of the constitution and all laws flowing therefrom.

What is needed is a law against the promulgation of the idea of Jihad. While Western society is loathe to limit the preaching of an idea, especially one based on religion, there is a compelling precedent in Europe for doing so. When an idea or concept becomes so abhorrent as to endanger society then its banishment from legitimate discourse becomes necessary. This was the case following the Second World War in Germany. National Socialism, as a political movement, and Nazism, based on racial supremacy, were outlawed. The concept of Jihad, the militant spread of Islam across the globe, can also be outlawed. Thus, supporting jihadist groups by collecting funds, spreading their propaganda, or indoctrinating mosque attendees, would be illegal. The government would also have the right to use intrusive law enforcement and intelligence techniques to ensure that the law was being obeyed. This law, by its nature, would almost exclusively be applicable only to Muslims, and would therefore be challenged in that regard. Anti-Nazi laws are generally only applicable to "Aryans," and have stood the test of time. The law could be similar in philosophy to the U.S. RICO statute, which prosecutes individuals not for a specific illegal act, but, for being part of a criminal conspiracy. The "offense" under the new law would be the support of Jihad, or conspiracy to engage in Jihad. This would not prohibit individual Muslims from believing in Jihad (as their religion demands), nor practicing "personal Jihad" in striving to be a better Muslim, but in acting in concert with others to propagate Jihad. Individual destructive acts could still be prosecuted under criminal and anti-terrorism laws. Deportations to countries where these acts are committed, or whose citizens have been harmed, must be allowed, regardless of the potential penalty that awaits the perpetrator. Without such a law, a patchwork of individual country laws that tries to contain "terrorism" will leave Europe as Jihad's incubator.

---

[225]"Mauritanian Government Arrests Islamic Militants for Alleged Coup Plotting," *Paris AFP World Service*, online ed., in English, 4 June 2003, URL: <*https://datawarehouse10.dia.ic.gov/fcgi-bin/webisdoc?DOC72D+316398+00000b7+repbrag*>, accessed on Intelink 4 June 2003.

THE U.S. INTELLIGENCE COMMUNITY
RESPONSE TO JIHAD

As explained earlier, the first response of the U.S. intelligence community (IC) to Jihad must be an enunciation of the strategic threat. In order to do this the IC must have individuals who can understand the nature of that threat. Frankly, this takes a more highly educated, trained, and probably intelligent analyst, than does dealing with operational and tactical issues. The strategic analyst must understand how an enemy thinks and is likely to react. He/she must be knowledgeable of the adversary's "world view" (in this case Islam), their history, culture, and language(s). If the enemies are jihadists, the IC needs "Jihad analysts." This is parallel to the situation during the Cold War when the IC had Soviet analysts who were knowledgeable about both the Soviet Union and communism. The IC now needs analysts with a deep understanding of Islam, and because Jihad is a global phenomenon, knowledge of regions where Muslim nations, and/or significant Muslim populations exist. It must be understood that the majority of the world's Muslims are not Arabs, and thus an "Arab centric" view of Islam is insufficient, and probably counterproductive. Since the social structure of many Muslim countries revolves around the family, clan, and tribe, the IC must gain knowledge of this sociological pattern. Gone are the days, especially of the 1970s, when discussion of tribal societies was frowned upon as being somehow demeaning to a particular group. The Tajik civil war and the U.S. involvement in Somalia served to highlight the importance of tribal allegiance. At first blush, the answer to the Community's needs for Jihad analysts may appear to lie in the academic institutions of America. These institutions, however, are not now equipped to provide a solution, as they have for decades been part of the problem.

There is a rich academic tradition, emanating from Europe, in the study of Islam. Early scholars were German, Hungarian, French, British, Russian, among others, who dedicated their lives to understanding Islam and its history. Because Islam is so diverse, knowledge of Arabic was insufficient, and these scholars tended to be linguists with in-depth knowledge of Persian and Turkish, in addition to Arabic.

> European writing on Islam from the sixteenth century onwards is of two main kinds, with two very different approaches. (1) The first of these is what one might call the scholarly, dominated by theology and philology, concerned primarily with the scriptures and with the classics of Islam. The Qur'an and the ancient Arabian literature were studied in the same way and by the same techniques as the Bible and the classics of Greece and Rome had been studied in Europe. The greatest attention was devoted to Arabic, somewhat less to Persian. Characteristically, hardly any attention at all was given to Turkish which, though it was the major language of the Muslim world at that time, had the disadvantage of being a living language and therefore, like English, French, and German, unworthy of serious scholarly attention. (2) A second group of writings was practical, concerned with the news from Turkey and, to a lesser extent, other Muslim countries.... This literature is based in the main

on direct observation and is intended to satisfy the need for accurate information about this dangerous yet interesting neighbor of Christendom.... During the nineteenth century European scholarship on Islam received a tremendous new impetus. Several new developments contributed to this great growth. One of these was the application to Islamic studies of the critical historical method which was being developed by European and especially German scholars for the study of Greek, Roman, and European history. The use of these methods for the study of the early history of Islam, the life of the Prophet, the foundation of the Caliphate, the great Arab conquests, and the like, carried these studies a major step forward and formed the basis for most subsequent writing, in the Islamic world as well as in Europe."[226]

A second important development was the emancipation of the European Jews and the consequent entry of Jewish scholars into the European universities. From the first, Jewish scholars made a major contribution to the development of Arabic and Islamic studies — a contribution which continues to this present day [1993], as far as politically-minded administrators and benefactors permit it.... Hebrew and Arabic are cognate languages, Judaism and Islam are sister religions, with many important resemblances between them. A Jew, particularly a learned Jew, had a head start over his Christian colleagues in the study of Islam and an immediacy of understanding which they could not easily attain.... Jewish scholars were among the first who attempted to present Islam to European readers as the Muslims themselves see it and to stress, to recognize, and indeed sometimes to romanticize the merits and achievements of Muslim civilization in its great days.[227]

Continuing the tradition of Western Islamic scholarship, U.S. universities should be capable of providing the IC with learned Islamic scholars. The problem is that the tradition of Islamic scholarship did not continue. As much else in the Middle East, it became a victim of the Arab, and more specifically, the Palestinian-Israeli conflict. Traditional Islamic scholarship was far from "Palestinian centric" and refused to view fourteen centuries of Islam through the politically expedient prism of "Palestinian rights." It also refused to limit itself to viewing Islam as solely an Arab issue. More crucial, Arab-Palestinian-centric "scholarship" was inconvenienced by the true history of the Muslim world, in which the Palestinians did not exist, and the historical tenets of Islam were tolerant of a Jewish, or for that matter a Christian (for centuries) presence in the Middle East. New "scholars" emerged at U.S. universities whose objective was political correctness and not historical accuracy. These scholars did not have the rich backgrounds in language and culture of traditional Western Islamic scholars. Often, their strongest credential was that they were Middle Eastern and/or Muslim.

---

[226]Lewis, *Islam in History*, 10-11.
[227]Lewis, *Islam in History*, 11-12.

First, the historian [and the intelligence analyst] must possess a scholarly knowledge of his subject. That is to say, in addition to the professional skills of the historian, he must be acquainted with the history, language, and culture of the people of whom he writes. In other fields to state this is to state the obvious, but unfortunately in Middle Eastern studies the point still needs to be emphasized. Professional advancement, success, and reputation in this area are compatible with a degree of ignorance and incompetence which would not be tolerated in other more developed fields of study. This led to low standards of entry, performance, and promotion in academic institutions and to the acceptance and acclamation as authorities, even as "standard works," of books of breathtaking superficiality and inaccuracy. Unfortunately such books are really "standard works" in the sense that they are cited, recommended, and even read by many people, in many places, for long periods.[228]

These new, Palestinian-centric scholars had to invent a new history of the Muslim world that created a "Palestinian people" and excluded Jews. The real history of Islam, as documented through many years of dedicated scholarship, was now "inconvenient," as were the scholars, now derisively termed "orientalists." They had to get rid of the witnesses, the "orientalists" whose scholarship on Islam and Muslim history far surpassed their own. Obviously, foremost among those scholars that had to be excluded from Middle East scholarship were Jews, who both traditionally excelled in those studies, and would certainly resist a Palestinian-centric, or Arab-centric, view of Islamic history.

In 1978, Edward Said, a professor of English and comparative literature at Columbia University, published a book entitled *Orientalism*. Said did not emerge from the ranks of Middle Eastern studies.... "Until the June 1967 war I was completely caught up in the life of a young professor of English," wrote Said. But "beginning in 1968, I started to think, write, and travel as someone who felt himself directly involved in the renaissance of Palestinian life and politics." So began a process of self-reinvention, as Said set out to establish his Palestinian identity.... In the years that followed, Said evolved into a public intellectual, meeting the growing American demand for a Palestinian perspective. Liberal opinion inside the media began to divide over Israel's policies after 1967, but split following the election of a rightist Israeli government in 1977.[229]

In *Orientalism*, Said situated the Palestinians in a much wider context. They were but the latest victims of a deep-seated prejudice against the Arabs, Islam, and the East more generally — a prejudice so systematic and coherent that it deserved to be described as "Orientalism," the intellectual and moral equivalent of anti-Semitism. Until Said, orientalism was generally understood

---

[228]Lewis, *Islam in History*, 55.
[229]Martin Kramer, *Ivory Towers on Sand* (Washington DC: The Washington Institute for Near East Policy, 2001), 27.

to refer to academic Oriental studies in the older, European tradition.... Said resurrected and re-semanticized the term, defining it as a supremacist ideology of difference, articulated in the West to justify its dominion over the East. Orientalism, according to Said, was racism of a deceptively subtle kind, and he sought to demonstrate its pervasiveness and continuity "since the time of Homer," but especially from the Enlightenment to the present. For most of this period, announced Said, "every European, in what he could say about the Orient, was a racist, an imperialist, and almost totally ethnocentric."[230]

According to Said:

Taking the late eighteenth as a very roughly defined starting point Orientalism can be discussed and analyzed as the corporate institution for dealing with the Orient — dealing with it by making statements about it, authorizing views of it, describing it, by teaching it, selling it, ruling over it: in short, Orientalism as a Western style for dominating, restructuring, and having authority over the Orient.[231]

My [Said's] contention is that Orientalism is fundamentally a political doctrine willed over the Orient because the Orient was weaker than the West, which elided the Orient's difference with its weakness.[232]

Said goes further, and viewing the U.S. as a successor to British and French regional imperialism, attributes Orientalism's vices to America. "The parallel between European and American imperial designs on the Orient (Near and Far) is obvious."[233]

In 1978 Said identified the negative relationship that existed between academia, the U.S. government and American industry involved in the Middle East. Unfortunately, Said and like-minded academics succeeded in destroying that relationship which they viewed as inherently evil.

There is of course a Middle East studies establishment, a pool of interests, "old boy" or "expert" networks linking corporate business, the foundations, the oil companies, the missions, the military, the foreign service, the intelligence community together with the academic world. There are grants and other rewards, there are organizations, there are hierarchies, there are institutes, centers, faculties, departments, all devoted to legitimizing and maintaining the authority of a handful of basic, basically unchangeable ideas about Islam, the Orient, and the Arabs.[234]

---

[230]Kramer, *Ivory Towers on Sand*, 28.
[231]Edward W. Said, *Orientalism* (New York: Pantheon Books, 1978), 3.
[232]Said, *Orientalism*, 204.
[233]Said, *Orientalism*, 295.
[234]Said, *Orientalism*, 301-302.

The destruction of the orientalist infrastructure in the U.S. leaves the Intelligence Community without the academic depth necessary to surge for the counter-Jihad.

Said's political opinions vis-à-vis the Palestinian-Israeli conflict would have remained just that, had his attack on traditional Islamic scholarship not led to a revolutionary change in the structure of U.S. academia.

> Most important of all, Said included scholarly orientalism in his scope, and even accorded it a crucial role in disseminating orientalist dogmas. This scholarship, claimed Said, validated and fed the popular orientalism of the poets, novelists, travelers, and painters. The self-image of the scholars as truth-seeking investigators was a fraudulent façade, behind which lurked a sordid tale of complicity with power and acquiescence in the idea of Western supremacy. Scholars willingly or inadvertently collaborated with European governments in the promotion and justification of empire-building in Arab and Muslim lands. None of them, even the most accomplished and well intentioned, could escape the corrupting effects of power upon knowledge. While other sciences advanced, scholarly orientalism remained an instance of arrested development. "Knowledge of the academic variety does not progress," concluded Said in 1981. "I think we should open knowledge to the non-expert."[235]

Unfortunately, academics of the "Saidian" school of Middle East studies not only failed to open knowledge, but sought to ignore it in the context of Islam. Knowledge of Islam is based upon history, ignoring that history, or more precisely failing to understand that history's very real impact on current trends, leads to errors in judgment that the Intelligence Community cannot afford to make.

> [I]n a PBS debate in 1977 [Mr. Said asserted] that the fourteen-centuries-old Islamic tradition and civilization are no more meaningful for the Arab world today than are seventh-century events in Europe for an understanding of present-day America.[236]

As evidenced by how fundamental Islamic tradition is to the modern jihadist, Said could not have been more mistaken. Had Said even cared to look at the works of the "discredited" orientalists, he would have known just how wrong he was. Even in 1910, orientalists identified the Wahabbi movement in Arabia as a force that looked toward the seventh century for inspiration. By 1977, Said should have been aware of this movement in Saudi Arabia and its potential impact on the Arab, and later the Islamic world. His PBS statement was driven by Said's concept of political reality, rather than knowledge.

> The utmost puritanical simplicity was reestablished, such as had been practiced, according to the testimony of hundreds of hadiths, by the Companions

---

[235]Kramer, *Ivory Towers on Sand*, 29.
[236]Lewis, *Islam and the West*, 117.

and even the Caliphs. All luxury was rejected. The conditions of seventh-century Medina were to serve, half a millennium later, as model and norm in the state the Wahhabis erected on the foundation of the sunna.[237]

As part of a lengthy attack on Bernard Lewis (Professor of Near Eastern Studies Emeritus at Princeton University), Said quotes Lewis as asserting in a *Commentary* article in 1976 that: "As the nationalist movement has become genuinely popular, so it has become less national and more religious — in other words less Arab and more Islamic."[238] Had Said paid more attention to the Orientalists' judgments, and less time attacking their scholarship, American academia may have been better positioned to provide the knowledge necessary for the government to have understood the brewing jihadist onslaught. Had U.S. academia been less concerned with issues of nationalism and colonial domination, they may have better understood the Pan-Islamic trend seething below the veneer of Westernization in the Middle East. Phillip Hitti in the 1960s best encapsulated the conflict in the Arab world between Pan-Arabism and Islam.

> The espousal of nationalism encouraged the principle of self-determination and both led to the struggle for independence from foreign rule. Meantime the new ideology from the West, with its stress on secular and material values and the importance it attaches to ethnic limitations and geographic boundaries, ran counter to the most cherished traditions of Islam, with its concepts of religious universality, political theocracy and exclusive sovereignty. Pan-Islam rather than Pan-Arabism would be the ideal toward which Moslems should strive. The conflict was on internal as well as external levels.[239]

Intelligence analysts must be taught the importance of Islamic history and culture, not simply modern Arab politics, a task that Saidian academics are ill-prepared to accomplish. "Orientalists in Europe and America have dealt with all the cultures of Asia — China and Japan, India and Indonesia; and in the Middle East their studies are by no means limited to the Arabs but have included the Turks and Persians as well as the ancient cultures of the region."[240] "His [Said's] Orient is reduced to the Middle East, and his Middle East to a part of the Arab world. By eliminating Turkish and Persian studies on the one hand and Semitic studies on the other, he isolates Arabic studies from both their historical and philological contexts. The dimensions of Orientalism in time and space are similarly restricted."[241] Even basic language skills, long recognized as essential for regional intelligence analysis, is given a sinister character by Said. "The acquired foreign language is therefore made part of a subtle assault upon populations, just as the study of a foreign region like the Orient is turned into a program of control by divination."[242]

---

[237]Goldziher, *Introduction to Islamic Theology and Law*, 244.

[238]Said, *Orientalism*, 317.

[239]Hitti, *History of the Arabs: From the Earliest Times to the Present*, 753.

[240]Lewis, *Islam and the West*, 115.

[241]Lewis, *Islam and the West*, 107-108.

[242]Said, *Orientalism*, 293.

An example of a greater depth of knowledge necessary to do proper analysis is the history of the spread of Wahabbi ideas. While Wahabbism, fueled by Saudi funding, has certainly been spreading in recent years, it has a relatively long history in Asia. Coming out of Arabia, for sure, but growing from its own roots in what was India, and is now India and Pakistan. Islamists in Pakistan, and in India, cannot be understood without this historical knowledge, lost to a modern Middle East scholar that ignores orientalist scholarship.

> Indian Islam has been experiencing such movements for the last hundred years. The ideas of the Wahhabi movement streamed out of Arabia into this Islamic land, as well. Contacts and experiences gained during the pilgrimage to Mecca have always proved a powerful means for the awakening of religious forces, for the adoption of new tendencies, and for their transplantation to remote areas of Islam. After a period of quiet theoretical preparation, the Wahabbi stimulus found in India a man who acted on it with vigor. This was Sayyid Ahmad Brelwi, who spread the Wahabbi ideas in the first quarter of the nineteenth century, in various regions of Muslim India.... In his zeal to bring back the early Islamic way of life, he also led his numerous followers into holy war, Jihad. Suppression of the Sikh sect, widespread in northern India...presented itself as an immediate aim. In this unsuccessful war he met his death, in 1831. Although the adventurous undertaking of the Jihad and the related political attempts came to an end with Ahmad's death, the intra-Islamic religious movement that he had set afoot continued to be effective in Indian Islam. Although not under the Wahabbi flag, the apostles of Ahmad's teachings worked in India, under various religious appellations, for the complete Islamization of the nominal Muslims who were still given to Indian practices. They won them over to the observance of Islamic law, and gathered bands of adherents to the sunna.[243]

It is one thing to limit one's scholarship by too focused a view. When personal attacks are launched against those with broader views and it impacts a field of study, a void of knowledge is created.

> And yet despite its failures, its lamentable jargon, its scarcely concealed racism, its paper-thin intellectual apparatus, Orientalism flourishes today [1978] in the forms I [Edward Said] have tried to describe.[244]

> This argument [orientalism as racist] also had practical implications. *Orientalism* appeared at a time when new minorities were seeking equitable if not preferential access to academe. Among them were Arabs and Muslims, for whom the field of Arab and Islamic studies had always been an obvious avenue for entry into the university. *Orientalism* gave them a step up. For who could escape the bind of orientalism, if not its ostensible victims, the Orientals themselves?...

---

[243]Goldziher, *Introduction to Islamic Theology and Law*, 257.
[244]Said, *Orientalism*, 322.

Middle Easterners, and especially Arab-Americans, had been in the first rank of the founders of Middle Eastern studies in America, and had long entered the university precisely through the Arab and Islamic field.... But they had not enjoyed automatic preference over others. *Orientalism* implicitly claimed for them a privileged understanding of the Arab and Islamic East, due not to any individual competence, but to their collective innocence of orientalist bias. They were unspoiled; they were entitled.[245]

In the more than twenty years since the publication of *Orientalism*, its impact on the broad intellectual climate in American Middle Eastern studies has been far-reaching. *Orientalism* made it acceptable, even expected, for scholars to spell out their own political commitments as a preface to anything they wrote or did. More than that, it also enshrined an acceptable hierarchy of political commitments, with Palestine at the top, followed by the Arab nation and the Islamic world....The political test included more than "right" and "wrong" in the Arab-Israeli dispute and extended to the entire range of American involvement in the Middle East....*Orientalism* not only overturned bookshelves, it overturned chairs. It became a manifesto of affirmative action for Arab and Muslim scholars and established a negative predisposition toward American (and imported European) scholars. In 1971, only 3.2 percent of Middle East area specialists had been born in the region.... "Our membership has changed over the years," announced MESA's [Middle East Studies Association] president in 1992, "and possibly half is now of Middle Eastern heritage."[246]

Since the mid-1970's the leaders of Middle East studies "...had argued against the erudite mastery of languages, histories, cultures, and societies. It was sufficient to come armed with the right theory, the most universally valid paradigm, and then apply it to the Middle East. The idea that there was anything exceptional about the Middle East was diagnosed as a symptom of 'latent' orientalism, a career-threatening affliction."[247] What is exceptional about the Middle East is that it is part of a broader Islamic world. Its history and culture did not start with European colonialism, and does not conform well to Western standards of states, and "church-state" relations. While a deeper understanding of historical and cultural factors could have led to better political analysis, non-Arab scholars were precluded by threat of being branded an "orientalist" from doing so. "This telling admission revealed much about the ethnic cleavage in Middle Eastern studies: only scholars of Middle Eastern origin could safely explore culture-based paradigms."[248] It was in the "culture-based paradigms" from which the modern Jihad sprung. Those academics that might have recognized the problem were precluded from doing so, those that were "allowed" to do so had other interests.

---

[245]Kramer, *Ivory Towers on Sand*, 33-34.

[246]Kramer, *Ivory Towers on Sand*, 37-39.

[247]Kramer, *Ivory Towers on Sand*, 109.

[248]Kramer, *Ivory Towers on Sand*, 79.

Modern Middle East academics generally lack the skills to compete with traditional oriental scholars. They also lack the objectivity necessary to seek historical truth. Thus, to gain dominance in the field, they had to change the rules.

> The hard-core philologist is an almost extinct species; those who believe that social, economic, political, and even literary theory may not only inform but also replace the study of sources continue to flourish. One of them, in a recent review of a work on Middle Eastern history, spoke of contempt of Orientalists who try to understand the history of another civilization by "the minute examination of difficult texts." In addition to indicating a well-attested preference for the superficial examination of easy texts, the remark illustrates a profound need to which anti-Orientalism provides a welcome relief. According to a currently fashionable epistemological view, absolute truth is either nonexistent or unattainable. Therefore, truth doesn't matter, facts don't matter. All discourse is a manifestation of a power relationship, and all knowledge is slanted. Therefore, accuracy doesn't matter; evidence doesn't matter. All that matters is the attitude — the motives and purposes — of the user of knowledge, and this may be simply claimed for oneself or imputed to another. In imputing motives, the irrelevance of truth, facts, evidence, and even plausibility is a great help. The mere assertion suffices. The same rules apply to claiming a motive; goodwill can be established quickly and easily by appropriate political support. This is demonstrated in *Orientalism,* in which scholars whose methods and procedures are indistinguishable by any scholarly or methodological criterion are divided into sheep and goats according to their support or lack of support for Arab causes. Such support, especially when buttressed by approved literary or social theories, can more than compensate for any lack of linguistic or historical knowledge.[249]

U.S. Middle East scholarship has been politicized. It was designed to create a "Palestinian people" where none had existed in history, establish Jerusalem as the "third holiest site in Islam" when it is not even mentioned in the Qur'an, and de-legitimize any Jewish claim to the area of "Palestine" which the Zionists had occupied as a vestige of European [now read American, (so what if it's not true)] colonialism. With "Palestine" as their top, and apparently only priority (why aren't the Kurds equally entitled to their own academic champions for a state?), U.S. Middle East scholarship, bolstered by their like-minded European colleagues, were highly successful in accomplishing their political objective, despite convoluted scholarship.

There is no doubt that today there is an Arab people that view themselves as "Palestinian." This is, however, a new-found identity, without historical roots. During World War Two a "Palestinian" was a Jew that lived in the British Palestine Mandate. Thus, the "Jewish Brigade" members of the British Army had the name "Palestine" on their uniforms. Had the founders of the modern Jewish state (after much debate) decided not to call the

---

[249]Lewis, *Islam and the West,* 114-115.

new state "Israel" but retained the name "Palestine" what would the Arab "Palestinians" be called today?

> In the depopulated Palestine of the eighteenth century the revenue from pilgrims constituted the main item. By the middle of that century the once fertile, sufficiently irrigated plains between Aleppo and the Euphrates had become what they are today, a desert. By the end of that century the entire population of Syria had estimatedly shrunk to about a million and a half, of whom perhaps less than a couple of hundred thousand lived in Palestine. Jerusalem in the early nineteenth century had an estimated population of 12,000...."[250]

It has even been argued, in a ridiculous attempt to give the "Palestinians" ancient roots in Israel, that they are descended from the biblical Canaanites, which, of course would make them not Arabs. For many years Arab states refused to recognize a separate "Palestinian" identity, preferring to term the Arabs living in that region either Jordanians, or southern Syrians.

Why is Jerusalem more holy to Islam than Karbala, or even Damascus, Baghdad, Cairo, or Istanbul (the latter four seats of Islamic Caliphates)? The simple answer is that it has to be in order to establish a Palestinian claim to the city that is the only holy city in Judaism. This claim is predicated on three modern notions. First that Al Aqsa is the "far mosque" referred to in the Qu'ran. Secondly, that Mohammad made his night journey to heaven from Jerusalem. Thirdly, that it was the first direction in which Muslims prayed. Surah 17, Al Isra (The Night Journey) or Bani Isra il (The Children of Israel), states that : Glory to (Allah) Who did take His Servant For a Journey by night From the Sacred Mosque To the Farthest Mosque."[251] According to a commentary on this surah:

> The Farthest Mosque must refer to the site of the Temple of Solomon in Jerusalem on the hill of Moriah, at or near which stands the Dome of the Rock. This and the Mosque known as the Farthest Mosque (al Masjid al Aqsa) were completed by the Amir 'Abd al Malik in A.H. 68. Farthest because it was the place of worship farthest west which was known to the Arabs in the time of the Holy Prophet: it was a sacred place to both Jews and Christians, but the Christians then had the upper hand, as it was included in the Byzantine (Roman) Empire, which maintained a Patriarch at Jerusalem.[252]

> The oldest surviving Muslim religious building outside Arabia, the Dome of the Rock in Jerusalem, was completed in 691 or 692 C.E. [Muhammed died in 632 C.E.]. The erection of this monument, on the site of the ancient Jewish temple, and in the style and the vicinity of Christian monuments such as the

---

[250]Hitti, *History of the Arabs: From the Earliest Times to the Present*, 728.
[251]Ali, *The Meaning of the Holy Qur'an*, 673.
[252]Ali, *The Meaning of the Holy Qur'an*, 673.

Holy Sepulcher and the Church of the Ascension, sent a clear message to the Jews and, more important, the Christians. Their revelations, though once authentic, had been corrupted by their unworthy custodians and were therefore superseded by the final and perfect revelation embodied in Islam.... To emphasize the point, the Qur'anic inscriptions in the Dome of the Rock denounce what Muslims regard as the principal Christian errors: "Praise be to God, who begets no son, and has no partner" and "He is one God, eternal. He does not beget, He is not begotten, and He has no peer" (Qur'an CXII). This was clearly a challenge to Christendom in its birthplace.[253]

The modern notion that Jerusalem is the third holiest site in Islam is a challenge to Judaism, at the site of its temple. After arriving in Medina, Muhammad did, in fact, have the faithful pray in the direction of Jerusalem, for a very short time.

He introduced Jerusalem as the direction to face during prayer (*kibla*) in the mosque he had built after his arrival; this is assumed although not stated explicitly in the Koran. After seventeen months [estimates differ], the direction was changed. Instead of Jerusalem (the name is not mentioned in the Koran), the Kaba in Mecca became the direction to be faced during prayer ([sura verse] 2:142-150)."[254]

Muhammad found it more expedient to direct prayers toward the Ka'aba in Mecca, and to therefore make it a religious obligation to conquer that city. While the Jews have never forgotten their only holy city, Jerusalem, it is strange that the Muslims, until it became expedient to do so, seem to have forgotten their "third holiest" city.

After the success of the Jihad and the recapture of Jerusalem, Saladin and his successors seem to have lost interest in the city, and in 1229 one of them even ceded Jerusalem to the emperor Frederick II as part of a general compromise agreement between the Muslim ruler and the crusaders. It was retaken in 1244, after the Crusaders tried to make it a purely Christian city. After a long period of relative obscurity, interest in the city was reawakened in the nineteenth century, first by the quarrels of the European powers over the custody of the Christian holy places, and then by the new Jewish immigration.[255]

It is interesting to note that Palestinians, such as Yasser Arafat, have now gone further, and deny the existence of the Jewish temple on Mount Moriah, claiming that it was elsewhere. Should Middle East scholars pick up that refrain, maybe they can also change Jewish, Christian, and Muslim history on this matter.

Modern Arab scholars seem to ignore the fact that the very same process that established the Arab states, begun after the breakup of the Ottoman Empire, also established

---

[253]Lewis, *The Crisis of Islam*, 43-44.
[254]Busse, *Islam, Judaism, and Christianity*, 19.
[255]Lewis, *The Crisis of Islam*, 50.

the State of Israel. If Israel was created as a result of colonialism, so was every Arab state. More properly, de-colonization left behind in the Middle East the modern notion of a nation state, which was an alien concept to Islam. Pan-Arabists, and now Pan-Islamists, seek to substitute a truer Muslim concept of an umma for the state system of the West. In the process they seek to eliminate the State of Israel, conceived from the same colonial past as the Arab states, but only having the potential of dhimmi status in the umma of Islam. While blaming the United States for "colonialism" in the Middle East is not historically accurate, it does serve the current purposes of the Palestinian-centric scholars who need a colonial scapegoat now that the true European colonial powers have long left the region.

Because of their myopic obsession with the Palestinian-Israeli issue, and the overwhelmingly large numbers of American scholars who were so focused, U.S. academe was, and is, ill-prepared to deal with the issue of Islam and Jihad. It is therefore, ill-prepared, and possibly incapable, of providing the Intelligence Community with the analysts needed to understand the war, or conduct a counter-Jihad.

> In retrospect, the new elite in Middle East studies had failed to ask the right questions, at the right time, about Islamism. They underestimated its impact in the 1980's; they misrepresented its role in the early 1990s; and they glossed over its growing potential for terrorism against America in the late 1990s. Twenty years of denial had produced mostly banalities about American bias and ignorance, and fantasies about Islamists as democratizers and reformers. These contributed to the public complacency about terrorism that ultimately left the United States vulnerable to "surprise" attack by Islamists. But there was no serious debate over Islamism within the field itself. Middle Eastern studies were so heavily invested in one interpretation that few dared to challenge the collective migration from one error to another. Dissent could be found only in think tanks that encouraged it, and in the Middle East itself, among intellectuals with a nearer and more acute angle of vision on Islamism in practice."[256]

Palestinian-centric scholarship led to the faulty "analysis" of the Middle East that ignored the global resurgence of militant Islam, and to Jihad as the central threat to the United States and its allies. Despite clear evidence in Iran, Lebanon, Tajikistan, Afghanistan, Chechnya, Pakistan, and to a lesser extent Somalia, of this Islamic/jihadist phenomenon, U.S. academia kept its eye on the prize of a Palestinian state, and remained unwilling, or unable, to come to grips with Jihad. In fact, U.S. academia, as represented by the Middle East Studies Association (MESA), did not include non-Arab Muslim regions within its areas of study. Therefore, the Jihad brewing in Central Asia, Africa, and Russia, was not likely to be scrutinized by a blinded academic organization.

---

[256]Kramer, *Ivory Towers on Sand*, 56-57.

But by the end of the 1990s, the institutions of Middle Eastern studies had failed to bring Caucasian and Central Asian studies under their umbrella. In part, this reflected the much more significant failure of Middle Eastern states to bring the region into their orbit. Scholars who predicted the emergence of a "greater Middle East" upon the breakup of the Soviet Union were disappointed. But it also reflected an underlying weakness in American-style Middle Eastern studies. That weakness showed itself in the inability of Middle East programs to keep even the Middle East under one academic umbrella.[257]

Not only may U.S. academia be unqualified to provide the IC with capable counter-Jihad analysts, but they have also shown a history of refusing to cooperate with the IC in Middle East studies. The Middle East Studies Association's reaction to the 1991 National Security Education Act sets the tone for academe's relationship to both the Department of Defense and the Intelligence Community. This program, designed to fund academic studies in support of the U.S. policy decisionmaking process, was run by the Department of Defense.

Not surprisingly, the National Security Education Program (NSEP) became a rallying point for academic radicals of every stripe. They again conjured up the image of intelligence agencies sending tentacles into the academy, and the mainstream area studies organizations mobilized to wrest the program from the Department of Defense.... MESA's resolutions during the controversy simply rehashed the themes of every past controversy. In 1992, it's Board of Directors "deplore[d] the location of responsibility [for the program] in the U.S. defense and intelligence community." This would "create dangers for students and scholars by fostering the perception of involvement in military or intelligence activities." MESA [wanted to] "ensure that the priorities, criteria, and funding goals of the program are developed from within the academic community," and that the program be guided by "university-based foreign area studies experts who have a wide-ranging and long-term view of national needs." [MESA meant its own leaders.] MESA ended by urging members and their institutions "not to seek or accept program or research funding" until the academics got their way.[258]

In 1995, MESA revealed the nefarious plot behind the NSEP: "'Congress intends to use the program to recruit young people into the intelligence services,' warned MESA's president,... 'by offering the tempting bait of fellowships at a time when scholarship funds are limited.'"[259]

On 19 June 2003, Stanley Kurtz, a research fellow at the Hoover Institution of Stanford University, and an anthropologist associated with South Asia, testified before the House

---

[257]Kramer, *Ivory Towers on Sand*, 112.
[258]Kramer, *Ivory Towers on Sand*, 94.
[259]Kramer, *Ivory Towers on Sand*, 95.

Subcommittee on Select Education on "Title VI fellowships" (federal funding of international studies). Specifically, Kurtz expounded on his critique of U.S. Middle East studies.

> His testimony argued that this field is dominated by an approach called post-colonial theory. Developed primarily by Edward Said of Columbia University, it holds, in Kurtz's words, that "it is immoral for a scholar to put his knowledge of foreign languages and cultures at the service of American power." The predominance of post-colonial theory had two major consequences: Exclusion of pro-American voices.... [and] [c]ondemnation of scholars who cooperate with the American government.[260]

According to Daniel Pipes, Director of the Middle East Forum: "Indeed, Kurtz understates the problem, for anti-Americanism among Middle East specialists has other sources besides post-colonial theory, such as fury at strong US-Israel relations or sympathy for the Iranian regime."[261]

What the IC needs to do is not "lure" those academics and students that are driven by a desire for fellowships, but to enlist in its ranks counter-Jihad warriors, armed with the knowledge and determination to win this war. It is for that reason that the IC cannot rely upon academia, and must establish a robust in-house education program for developing future analysts. In addition, the IC needs Islamic/Jihad analysts and not merely Middle East studies students, for this purpose. This program should be modeled on the now-defunct Soviet Foreign Area Officer program of the United States Army. The Army program combined academic and government education over a four-year period, producing officers who understood the nature of the enemy (language, culture, history, politics) but were not fellow travelers. They used their knowledge to defeat the enemy, not empathize with him.

In addition to analysis to support political decisions, the Intelligence Community must now be prepared to support counter-Jihad initiatives that include: the neutralization of individual or small groups of jihadists; larger-scale special operations forces (SOF) missions in permissive and non-permissive environments; "peacekeeping" missions; and force-on force conventional combat. Key to the success of the IC will be a cadre of knowledgeable "all-source" analysts, supported by highly skilled technical analysts working in a "multi-int" (multiple intelligence collection sources) environment. No single source of intelligence collection is sufficient to provide the needed actionable intelligence, nor is the emphasis between the disciplines going to be the same in each instance. Sources are rarely "perfect" and almost always need to be corroborated and should seldom be used on their own for action. Geospatial Intelligence (formerly IMINT and geospatial) is accurate on its own in many situations, especially in force-on-force conventional combat, but has a more limited stand-alone utility in other support missions. Multi-int analysis offers, therefore, the most-promising guidance for future U.S. intelligence collection. Integration of collection and

---

[260]Daniel Pipes, "Wasted Money," *New York Post*, online ed., 24 June 2003, URL: <http//www.nypost.com/cgi-bin/printfriendly.pl>, accessed 24 June 2003.
[261] Pipes, "Wasted Money."

analysis must, however, be timely and be presented to the "all-source" analyst in a coherent manner. "Stovepipe" analysts must work collaboratively, and include a relatively refined working knowledge of each other's tradecraft. "All-source" analysts must learn how to use the information provided by the fusion of the "stovepipes" and how to use that greater degree of information to analyze the Jihad puzzle.

The IC, in its new-found relationship with law enforcement, and its history of support to "counterterrorism" must not fall into the analytic trap of seeking the types of linkages of individuals and groups that is common in terrorism analysis and law enforcement. Law enforcement, worldwide, relies upon establishing an organization as a named "terrorist" group. It then seeks to prosecute members of that group, and associated groups. But Jihad is Jihad, by whatever name. The names change often, and the linkages are tenuous. "Card carrying" members of Al-Qa'ida are hard to find. Thus, fighting an organization is not possible. It is the jihadist's belief in Jihad that makes him a threat, not membership in an organization. Cooperation among jihadists is of a strategic, and not operational or tactical nature. They all are fighting for the same cause, and thus provide ongoing and interwoven support (financial, material, safe haven, personnel) to each other. This is not equivalent to the cooperation exhibited in the 1970s between terrorist groups with fundamentally different agendas. Thus, support that Al-Qa'ida receives from, or gives to, other jihadists, in no way resembles the attack on Lod airport, where members of the Japanese Red Army attacked an airport in Israel, killing American tourists from Puerto Rico, at the behest of the PLO.[262] For law enforcement reasons having to do with gaining international cooperation and invoking general and extradition treaties, and freezing of funding, the U.S. government on a political/law enforcement level may deem it valuable to characterize jihadists as terrorists; the Intelligence Community cannot afford to do so.

Intelligence analysts must break away from stereotypical thinking that is common in terrorism analysis. In counter-Jihad analysis, not only are the linkages and relationships different, but so is the motivation, and thus likely actions. For example, the publicity paradigm of terrorism must now be turned on its head. Conventional analysis held that a terrorist group would not conduct operations that would be detrimental to its cause in world opinion. This is generally true of terrorist groups that seek to pressure the international community to support their aims, while not going too far in alienating their audience. Jihadists, however, play to a different audience. Their major concern is striking massive blows at their enemies both to inflict maximum damage, and to energize their "audience" of Muslims worldwide into joining the Jihad. Impediments to operations are not world opinion, but religious objections (most of which are readily overcome) and negative reactions in donor nations (also ignored when action is needed). The analysis of the smallpox threat is an interesting case in point. This was never an issue when dealing with 1970s terrorists, even those associated (as most were) with the Soviet Union and/or East Germany, and thus potentially having access to biological weapons. It was expected that there would be no benefit to the goals of these groups to develop and/or use such weapons.

---

[262]"What Happened at the Lod Airport in 1972?," Palestine Facts, URL: *http://www.palestine-facts.org/pf_1967to1991_lod_a1972.php*, accessed January 2004.

Analyzing Al-Qa'ida's desire to inflict mass casualties on the U.S. (and Jews), it was determined that in fact a smallpox threat existed. This, however, was only a partial analysis. A full analysis, and understanding of the threat of Jihad, would lead to the conclusion that this was not a viable Al-Qa'ida option. Unleashing an epidemic, while potentially killing millions, was uncontrollable. It was in fact more likely that millions of Muslims, without access to vaccines and treatment, would ultimately be killed. Deaths in the U.S. would proportionately be considerably fewer. A U.S. announcement of this fact would have been sufficient to ameliorate this threat, if there ever was one. Al-Qa'ida needs "spectacular" successes against the U.S. and Jews, not unleashing a global epidemic for which they could not take credit as millions of Muslims died, or became dependent on the West or the U.S. to save their lives.

Considering intelligence appropriate to counter-terrorism to be the same as that to counter-Jihad leads to prioritizing collection and analysis based upon specific groups. Some must be deemed more dangerous, and thus a higher priority, than others. Jihad, though, must be analyzed equally across the spectrum of all groups, individuals, non-governmental organizations (NGOs), and governmental agencies that support it in any manner. Cooperation among jihadists is fluid, with group affiliation meaning little. Thus, intelligence priorities for a given group may be lower than the actual threat of that group as it interacts and plans operations in conjunction with, or in support of other jihadists. This will lead to "surprises" as a low-priority jihadist group conducts a "spectacular" operation. More importantly, by viewing jihadists as a compilation of separate groups and organizations, the Intelligence Community will fail to understand the overarching threat of the Jihad directed against the United States. The synergy between jihadist operatives and their support structure in NGOs, mosques, Islamic centers, and governments will be lost as these entities receive differing IC emphases. Even as it continues its counterterrorism focus, the IC must establish a well-thought-out structure for giving its highest emphasis to support the counter-Jihad. The first step is separating the two issues; the second is to recognize and collect against the total Islamic/jihadist structure.

All intelligence collection is worthless if it is not properly analyzed, then synthesized. Intelligence Community counter-Jihad analysts must be developed that can put the puzzle together. This will not be an easy task, and the IC will receive little help from U.S. academia. The process of developing these analysts will take years. So also will the Jihad persist that is being waged against America. Fortunately, the IC has a unique tool to aid in this battle. The Joint Military Intelligence College (JMIC), hosted by the Defense Intelligence Agency, if properly focused, can serve as an incubator for developing counter-Jihad analysts. The mission, however, must be clear: It is not counterterrorism, although this will accompany the initial focus on producing analysts with insight into Jihad. A longer-range program, involving traditional foreign area skills in language (not only Arabic but all the languages of Islam), religion, culture, history, and in-country training, can be developed in select academic institutions, initially in coordination with the JMIC, and eventually as a stand-alone institution similar to the now-defunct U.S. Army Russian Institute. As always, failure to understand the enemy will lead to costly mistakes. In an age of Al-Qa'ida and sympathetic jihadists globally, the U.S. can afford few mistakes.

THE OPERATIONAL THREAT

Al-Qa'ida planners and operators are not "ten feet tall." Although the 9/11 attacks had spectacular results, representing the apparent ability to overcome huge operational challenges, the success of Al-Qa'ida was arguably based on fortuitous circumstances rather than operational expertise. Other Al-Qa'ida operations were not so lucky, with many not being executed, and others, seemingly successful, in reality were not. The initial, 1993 (pre-dating the formation of Al-Qa'ida) attack on the World Trade Center was both poorly planned and executed. Even though damage was done, it was far less severe than it might have been. The attack on the Pentagon, although a terrible loss of life, was not ultimately significant, and the fourth target was never hit. The *USS Cole* was successfully attacked, but was not sunk. The U.S. Embassy bombings in Kenya and Tanzania were highly successful, as explosions, but killed few Americans and many locals (including Muslims). The Dzerba synagogue attack killed no Jews, but many Germans. The French Tanker Limburgh, although damaged, neither exploded nor sank. The 19 May 2003 attacks in Casablanca, Morocco occurred on a Friday night. The Jewish Sabbath, on Saturday, actually begins at sundown on Friday night, thus the targeted "Jewish Alliance Club" was closed. No Jews died in the Morocco attacks. The attack on the Israeli-owned Paradise Hotel in Mombassa, Kenya, and the concomitant attack on the Israeli Arkia airliner at Mombassa Airport, were almost complete failures. Although any deaths are regrettable, only three Israelis were killed. The suicide bomber attacked the hotel lobby after most Israelis had departed. The Arkia airliner was not hit. The attack on the Paradise could have been a large success. Instead, poor execution and training resulted in what can only be termed a botched operation. The Casablanca attacks provided a very low ratio of suicide bombers to victims (only up to 1:2.5). This is far from an "efficient" use of suicide bombers.

Al-Qa'ida and other jihadists may not be ten feet tall, but they are certainly very dangerous. They prefer to target U.S. and Jewish presence overseas, and the U.S. economy in CONUS. They have declared Jihad against the U.S., against Jews, and in particular against New York City, where their targets "come together." They are marked by their tenacity, willingness to endure hardship, and sacrifice. They constantly attempt to formulate plans to kill as many Americans and Jews as possible. When it is not possible to combine their three objectives, separate planning to disrupt the U.S. economy occurs. A fixation on the U.S. economy likely comes from a continuing Muslim belief that the reason for Western dominance over Islam is a result of a strong economy and industry. This belief goes back to the Ottoman Empire, which attempted to analyze its weakened military position vis-à-vis Europe.

> [T]hey looked for the secret of Western success in those features of the West that were most distinctive, most different from anything in their own experience — and not tainted with Christianity.... For the whole of the nineteenth and most of the twentieth century the search for the hidden talisman concentrated on two aspects of the West — economics and politics, or to put it

differently, wealth and power. The economy, and more especially industry, was seen as the prime source of wealth and therefore ultimately of military effectiveness.[263]

Jihadists are very media-savvy. They realize, as did the Nazis, that the best propaganda is visual. The proliferation of compact video tape, and now digital cameras, coupled with the capability to present the images on tape, television, and the Internet, is a powerful recruiting, fundraising, and "morale" tool. If the Iranian Revolution in 1979 was a "cassette-tape revolution," then the modern Jihad is a video one. This practice, along with suicide bombings, was learned from Hizballah in Lebanon, where they usually videotaped their "operations" against the Israeli Army and/or Army of South Lebanon. Video allows for both selective editing and misleading voiceovers, making the audience believe that they are actually "seeing" what you are telling them they are seeing. Al-Qa'ida has made good use of this technique in filming their "victories" in Afghanistan, Chechnya, and elsewhere, without showing the full extent of the fighting. This leaves the would-be jihadist eager to join the obviously easy Muslim victories, without seeing the disproportionate casualties suffered. Al-Qa'ida also uses Western news footage, re-edited, and provided with an Arabic voiceover (which may not at all resemble what was originally said) in their videos.

In addition to using videos of Islamic "victories" to motivate recruits, the jihadists also use videos of Muslims being "oppressed" for fundraising and inciting rage. These videos are carefully edited, and are often taken from Western or Arab TV, to show Muslims suffering in "Palestine" at the hands of the Jews (there is no such person as an Israeli), Chechens suffering at the hands of the Russians, or Afghans and Iraqis (preferably children) being killed/maimed by Americans. Sympathetic Muslim journalists, and unwitting Western ones, often aid in this endeavor.

> The Western allies heavily bombed what they call "emerging targets' in Afghanistan. Western military commanders frequently repeat this statement, "...these pockets of resistance are determined to fight to the death; we would be happy to oblige them!" However, this is not called violence and barbarism, even though it indoctrinates [sic] the very statement Islam is being criticized for, that is, "kill them wherever you find them."[264]

The free U.S. media is good at identifying so-called U.S. vulnerabilities. In addition, political and economic analysts are more than happy to notify Al-Qa'ida of the potential impact of certain types of operations (another large scale 9/11 type attack) on the U.S. economy and the U.S. presidential race. Over-hyping events such as the post 9/11 anthrax attack, and the 2002 sniper attacks in the Washington D.C. area, serve to provide Al-Qa'ida with useful insights. Over-reporting of potential threats also gives Al-Qa'ida operatives the impression that America "fears" certain types of attacks, such as a nuclear

---

[263]Lewis, *What Went Wrong*, 46.
[264]Abualrub, *Holy War Crusades Jihad: In the Torah, the Gospels, and the Quran*, 138-139.

"dirty bomb." This perception of American "fear" could lead them to emphasize such operations. It is also convenient for the jihadists that U.S. media, and the Intelligence Community, do them the favor of authenticating supposed messages from their leaders. Providing scientific analysis of the results of their attacks, such as the heating of the metal beams in the World Trade Center as the reason for its collapse, would lead to increased and better planning against similar targets. The defense that Al-Qa'ida knows all this, or that it is in the public domain (if you happen to be an expert on certain vulnerabilities) is a poor excuse.

Loyalty in the Muslim, but especially the Arab world, flows from the individual, to the family, to the clan, and to the tribe. Tribal loyalty, in all instances, is above loyalty to the Western concept of a "nation state" that has been imposed upon Islam. Since tribal boundaries, sometimes nomadic, sometimes fixed, do not adhere to national borders, tribal connections are critical in "overcoming" those borders. Because of greater tribal loyalty than national loyalty, many governments have little or no control over their borders. In many instances governments rely upon tribal support, and thus do not have the wherewithal to force the tribes to adhere to government policies. Tribes adhere to ancient traditions of loyalty and hospitality, and thus are likely to continue to support their own members, or those with whom they have established bonds. Jihadists fully understand this tribal culture and use it to their advantage. Jihadist cells often contain relatives. Recruitment within a family group, clan or tribe is easier and more secure. Relatives and tribal members in government can provide valuable intelligence to, and intervene on behalf of, jihadists. Tribal lands form a ready "logistics" base from which to operate. Although jihadists don't often come from the country in which they are fighting, they are able to "cement" relationships with local tribes by marrying into them. Ultimately, however, tribal leaders will do what they perceive to be in the best interests of their tribe.

Can the Islamic world, divided into Shi'a and Sunni, be united in Jihad? Traditionally, the answer has been no. However, the modern Jihad may be blurring centuries of historical animosities and returning to shared roots. This trend is evident in Mosques in Europe and Latin America.

> In earlier times, the divisions between Sunni and Shi'a and between the many groups among the Shi'a were not as rigid as they later became; they were never, even later, as rigid as the differences between Protestants and Catholics or even between the different Protestant churches in Christendom. To the present day, the difference is strongly felt only in countries like Iraq, Lebanon, and Pakistan, where Sunni and Shi'a communities live side by side. Among Muslims in both Arab and black Africa and in Southeast Asia, where Shi'ites are little known, the difference is of far less importance, and Shi'ite leaders can win Sunni followers. In the earlier period especially, movement was easy from one to the other. And when seen from a Sunni point of view, even Shi'ism is not necessarily a religious aberration, a theological deviation. Sunni jurists and theologians have

sometimes been willing to consider moderate Shi'a views as falling within the permitted limits of difference of opinion.[265]

The main difference between Sunnis and Shi'a is not one of religious doctrine or authority. It is in origin a disagreement between parties on a political issue, about who should be the head of state, and by what right. The word Shi'a in Arabic means party and refers to the Shi'at 'Ali, those who believed that "Ali as kinsman of the Prophet should be his successor as Caliph and head the community. The two groups developed along different lines, but the differences are primarily of experience, of emotion and attitudes rather than of doctrine or belief."[266]

The West, therefore, cannot rely on a "wall" between Shi'a and Sunni to mitigate the threat.

While Shi'as and modern Sunni jihadists may disagree on many issues, they do have two things greatly in common. Both view current Sunni Muslim governments as illegitimate, and both strive for global imposition of shari'a. "In view of the greater task of winning over the world of unbelievers for Islam, the Shi'ites were (and are) willing to put aside denominational differences between them and the Sunnis."[267] Recent instances of Shi'a-Sunni solidarity include the handing over of the Israeli Embassy in Tehran to Yasser Arafat and the PLO by Khomeini after the Islamic revolution, Hizballah-Hamas ties, and the convergence of interests between the Sunni Muslim Brotherhood and Shi'a Islamists of the late 1940s and early 1950s.

The Muslim Brothers and their successors were in the main confined to the Arabic-speaking countries. But there were other parallel movements elsewhere. In Iran this trend was for a while represented by an organization called the Fida'iyan-I Islam (Devotees of Islam). This group was active mainly in Tehran between 1943 and 1955 and carried out a number of political assassinations, the most important being that of the prime minister, General 'Ali Razmara, in March 1951. The Devotees had some impact on Iranian politics, until another, this time unsuccessful, attempt on the life of the Prime Minister, Hossein 'Ala, in October 1955, led to their suppression and prosecution and the execution of some of their leaders. The Devotees had links with the Brothers and exercised considerable influence among the masses and, through terror, on politicians."[268]

While the Shi'a may not have yet fully joined the modern Jihad, they will lend it support.

---

[265]Lewis, *Islam and the West*, 156.

[266]Bernard Lewis, *The Multiple Identities of the Middle East* (New York: Schocken Books, 1998), 126.

[267]Busse, *Islam, Judaism, and Christianity*, 156.

[268]Lewis, *Islam and the West*, 141.

There is no Muslim state that adheres strictly to shari'a. Both the Taliban attempt in Afghanistan, and the Mullah's attempt in Iran, met or are meeting with opposition both within and externally. Therefore, all Muslim governments are open to the charge that they do not rule strictly according to shari'a. Even the "puritanical" al-Saud are open to this charge. Opposition to shari'a, however, is viewed (rightly in theory) as opposition to Islam. It is a charge well used by jihadists, and it cannot be readily refuted. To govern strictly by shari'a is impossible; for a government to acknowledge that it is not doing so is un-Islamic. Compounding this problem is a lack of religious hierarchy in Islam that can lend legitimacy to a government. Therefore, each Muslim government is left to "control" the jurists within their own country. Unfortunately, jihadist imams tend to be charismatic, and carry a simple and assertive message that resonates with a willing audience, in contrast with the "official" Islamic establishment. The jihadist deals with a single message: the oppression of the Muslims by outside forces which requires a defensive Jihad on the part of all of the faithful. These claims are bolstered by images of Muslims under attack on global battlefields. Counter-arguments are complex and not likely well understood by the masses.

COUNTER-JIHAD CENTERS OF GRAVITY

Jihad has existed since the advent of Islam fourteen hundred years ago. It is central to the religion, but was seen as only a "temporary" necessity until the world recognized the Prophet and Islam. The fact that it is still ongoing can of itself be seen as a failure of Islam. "The Jihad, it will be recalled, was regarded as Islam's instrument to transform the dar al-Harb into dar al-Islam. If that end had been achieved, the dar al-Harb would have been reduced to nonexistence, and the *raison d'etre* of the Jihad, except perhaps for combating Islam's internal enemies, would eventually have disappeared."[269] The modern Jihad is a manifestation of fourteen hundred years of failure.

Jihad has three fundamental centers of strategic gravity: overwhelming military opposition; Islamic jurisprudence; concern for family (a subset being the role of women). An emphasis on all three will result in both the loss of faith in, and the desire to conduct, Jihad. In all three areas the West must demonstrate both resolve, and steadfast determination to convince the Muslim umma to take the steps necessary to undermine the modern Jihad.

Even though Muslims have created great empires, and up to one-fifth of the world's population adhere (in varying degrees) to that religion, Jihad has not accomplished its purpose. It has expanded when faced by weakness, but has contracted when faced by superior force. Prolonged periods of military inferiority have "sapped the strength" of Jihad, and left Muslims without the energy to continue to attempt to forcibly expand their domination. The laws of Jihad have, in fact, been altered to accommodate this reality. During periods of opposition weakness, or lack of opposition, Jihad, still a very potent part of Islam, has been reenergized. Thus, when Arab-Muslim Jihad exhausted itself, the Turkish-Muslim Jihad, energized by its new faith and military prowess, expanded the borders of Islam. It was not until the Ottoman Turks militarily exhausted themselves against superior European and Russian forces that the last great Jihad ended.

The Ottoman was the last great cohesive Islamic empire with the capability to expand its borders. Today, there is no Muslim state that can unite Islam in a single great empire, energize the forces of Jihad, and continue Muslim conquests. What has replaced empire-building in the modern era is building an "empire" of like-minded people, across national boundaries, with like ideals and objectives. In Europe, this is manifesting itself in the liberal European Union, encompassing an increasing group of fairly conservative independent states. In Islam, the ready vehicle for uniting Muslims in a single cause was built into the religion by Muhammad: Jihad. Jihad, as both an idea and a call to action, will continue to grow, as does an empire, until it meets a countervailing and superior force. Thus, the single most important strategic center of gravity to counter Jihad is "military" defeat. Jihad draws energy from victories, however small, and loses momentum from a constant stream of defeats. As the Egyptians were able to "convince"

---

[269]Khadduri, *War and Peace in the Law of Islam*, 141.

their jihadists, by unrelenting physical pressure, to abstain from armed Jihad, the global Jihad can be "convinced" the same way. As a self-preservation measure Islam has developed circumstances whereby Jihad must be suspended. This "self-preservation measure" must be forced to be "activated." Global Jihad must be confronted globally; local Jihads must be eliminated locally. The success of any Jihad, anywhere, will fuel Jihad everywhere. As the disintegration of the Soviet Union, and Muslim victories in the Balkans, and Somalia, provided jihadists with a great impetus in the 1990s, so a Muslim victory against Russia today, with the potential of splitting that country and unleashing a Muslim resurgence not seen since the Tatars, would energize global Jihad. Conversely, a Muslim defeat at the hands of the Russians would be a devastating blow to Islamists, not only in the Caucasus, but in Central Asia, and to jihadists globally.

Since Jihad is a religious obligation, governed by religious law and jurisprudence, fatwas are essential to jihadists. While jihadists can, and do, ignore and ridicule rulings by "moderate" Islamic scholars, they cannot, and do not, ignore fatwas that have universal support, or come from jurists that generally support Jihad. Particularly of concern is a contrary ruling from a jurist upon whose authority they are conducting their Jihad. Consistently negative rulings (fatwas) from "radical" jurists, coupled with a general disapproval by the umma (the Muslim nation), will dry up support and volunteers. Even senior leaders, if unable to argue against criticism with learned fatwas of their own, will be given pause. "The classical jurists distinguish clearly between facing certain death at the hands of the enemy and killing oneself by one's own hand. The one leads to heaven, the other to hell. Some recent fundamentalist jurists and others have blurred or even dismissed this distinction, but their view is by no means unanimously accepted. The suicide bomber is thus taking considerable risk on a theological nicety."[270] There are actions that Muslims can take to more than mutely verbalize their disapproval of suicide bombers. The umma must stop celebrating suicides. Instead of the suicide being celebrated as a "martyr," as did Mohammad, they should not attend the funeral. A sustained show of disapproval by the Muslim community can limit the attraction of becoming a suicide bomber. A suicide's family, instead of celebrating their relative's passage to paradise (where he can intercede on their behalf) should mourn his potential journey to hell.

The final strategic center of gravity is the jihadist's family. Celebration of "martyrdom" reinforces the jihadist's family's stature in the community. Martyrdom of a relative, or even participation in Jihad, brings continuing esteem and financial reward. The jihadist cares for his family, and is religiously obligated, as are his fellow jihadists if something happens to him, to provide for their material welfare. Today, the jihadist is assured that his family will be taken care of. Minus that assurance, the ranks of jihadists will decrease. Suicide bombers' families in Israel will no longer get their stipend from Iraq. Assuring that a suicide bomber, or wanted/incarcerated families of jihadists are left in dire financial conditions, will have a dampening effect on Jihad.

---

[270]Lewis, *The Crisis of Islam*, 38-39.

Related to a jihadist's concern for his family are the larger issue of the family structure and the role of the male as head of the household. Potentially the greatest strategic center of gravity is the role of women in Islam. Should that role fundamentally change, and "modernize," Muslim society will be transformed. Attempts to change society at the household level must be carefully considered. What the West would view as the "liberation" of women will be viewed by most of the Muslim world, men and women, as an attack on Islam at its very core. The "liberation" of Muslim women must be the result of societal change, and not be its driver. That said, with careful analysis of a particular Muslim region, it should be possible to accelerate a change in women's status as an impetus to modernization and religious reform.

> According to Islamic law and tradition, there were three groups of people who did not benefit from the general Muslim principle of legal and religious [e]quality — unbelievers, slaves, and women. The woman was obviously in one significant respect the worst-placed of the three. The slave could be freed by his master; the unbeliever could at any time become a believer by his own choice, and thus end his inferiority. Only the woman was doomed forever to remain what she was — or so it seemed at the time.[271]

Western pressure eventually forced an official end to slavery in 1962 (not without religious objection that to end slavery was un-Islamic), and brought protections to non-dhimmi Westerners living in Muslim countries. "The struggle for women's rights proved much more difficult, and the outcome of that struggle is far from clear."[272] "It is surely significant that one of the most widely and frequently repeated grievances of the Muslim fundamentalists is the emancipation of women and the consequent damage to propriety and decency."[273]

Of the two Muslim states that attempted to legally emancipate women, one was turned into an Islamic republic, and the other has been under almost constant pressure from its Muslim populace.

> This [the abolition of shari'a law] is of particular concern to two groups which had, in law at least, benefited most from the reforms, namely women and non-Muslims. Hence the phenomenon, paradoxical in Western but not Muslim eyes, that such conventionally liberal causes as equal rights for women have hereto been espoused and enforced only by autocratic rulers like Kemal Ataturk in Turkey and Mohamed Reza Shah in Iran. For the latter, this was one of the main grievances of the revolutionaries who overthrew him. It has been remedied under their rule.[274]

---

[271]Lewis, *What Went Wrong*, 67-69.

[272]Lewis, *What Went Wrong*, 69.

[273]Lewis, *Islam in History*, 417.

[274]Lewis, *Islam in History*, 271.

The Ayatollah Khomeini, in particular, gave it [the emancipation of women] a prominent place in his indictment of the misdeeds of the shah and the crimes of the regime. From a traditional point of view, the emancipation of women — specifically, allowing them to reveal their faces, their arms, and their legs, and to mingle socially in the school or the workplace with men — is an incitement to immorality and promiscuity, and a deadly blow to the very heart of Islamic society, the Muslim family and home.[275]

It is unlikely that there is widespread support in any Muslim country for the functional emancipation of women, even among the majority of females. There are certainly, in all Muslim countries, women who would lead and support such a movement. A nineteenth-century example occurred in Persia, whereas in the twentieth century a short-lived period of legal emancipation existed in the modern state of Iran.

In Persia, neither foreign critics nor Muslim liberals and reformers showed much interest in woman's rights, but Persian women themselves began the fight for emancipation. A notable figure was Qurrat al-Ayn (1814-1852), the eldest daughter of an eminent Shi'ite Muslim theologian. She appears to have received a good Islamic education, but became an active follower of the Bab, the famous Islamic reformer who created what was virtually a new religion [without a belief in Jihad] in nineteenth-century Persia. Among other offences, she preached without a veil and denounced polygamy. She was martyred, along with at least 27 other Babis, and was put to death by torture.[276]

The strategic center of gravity for counter-Jihad is not the opening of a limited number of opportunities for women in the economy or government of Muslim countries. It is the fundamental change to Islam that would result from the full emancipation of over fifty percent of the population, and the breaking down of the male ethos in Islam that drives Jihad. The evidence of this fundamental change will not lie among female doctors, educators, lawyers, politicians, or NGO employees. It will be in the villages, where young girls are being fully educated (not just with an Islamic curriculum), and where women leave the house and participate in the running of local/village affairs. Emancipation of women in the Muslim world is not a national, but an Islamic issue. Today, the vast majority of Muslim women do not likely see themselves as "oppressed," but rather protected by Islam.

While there are numerous *operational* centers of gravity that can be employed to lessen the impact of Jihad, attacking one, or all of them, will not have the desired effect without attacking the *strategic* centers of gravity. In conjunction with attacking the strategic centers of gravity, the most obvious and highest-priority, operational center of gravity is funding. There is no doubt that money is necessary for modern Jihad. The problem, however, is that as long as Muslims have funds, and as long as the vast majority supports the concept of Jihad, money will flow to the jihadists.

---

[275]Lewis, *What Went Wrong*, 70.
[276]Lewis, *What Went Wrong*, 94-95.

In addition to communication facilitated by travel, modern communication methods, to include cell and satellite phones, as well as the Internet, are essential in facilitating a global Jihad. At the same time, for Jihad to succeed in attracting adherents requires an Islamic emphasis on hatred of the West and Jews, and that Jihad be taught in the Mosques and madrassas. As long as Muslim rulers view this as benign, and the West considers such preaching "religious freedom," Jihad will flourish. What goes on in a Mosque, in a madrassa, or on an Islamic radio or television broadcast, as many Arab governments recognize, can constitute a threat. "Islamic movements also have another immense advantage as contrasted with their competitors. In the Mosques they dispose of a network of association and communication that even the most dictatorial of governments cannot entirely control."[277] This advantage is enhanced in the West by an extreme reluctance to "interfere" in Mosque activities, even when these activities are promoting Jihad.

> [T]his privileged immunity has been extended, de facto, to Western countries where Muslim communities are now established and where Muslim beliefs and practices are accorded a level of immunity from criticism that the Christian majorities have lost and the Jewish minorities never had.... Islam is not only a matter of faith, and practice; it is also an identity and a loyalty — for many, an identity and loyalty that transcend all others.[278]

Jihadist centers of gravity are numerous and identifiable. Strategic intelligence analysts with the understanding to identify and exploit these centers of gravity must be available to the IC. The military dimension to the counter-Jihad must be supplemented with a vigorous and simultaneous, asymmetric attack on those centers. Influencing the strategic centers of gravity through the development of novel approaches will make the jihadists vulnerable at both the operational and tactical level.

---

[277]Lewis, *The Crisis of Islam*, 23.
[278]Lewis, *The Crisis of Islam*, 17.

CONCLUSION

Islam is in a period of advancement and expansion. Not only is it gaining new adherents, but there is an Islamic awakening among Muslims who have long either quietly or only nominally followed their religion. With the fall of the Soviet Union the opportunity now exists for millions of Muslims, whose faith was suppressed by atheist communists, to rejoin the Muslim world. The energy for this expansion is coming from the dynamic combination of the Wahhabi brand of Islam and Saudi/Gulf States' oil wealth. This period of Islamic activism comes at a time when the traditional bulwarks to Muslim expansion, Europe and Russia, are no longer able, or willing, to fulfill that role. Russia is acutely aware of the threat that could cut the nation in half, but is militarily, politically, and economically unable to respond effectively. Europe, looking toward an alternate future of unity, prosperity, and the rule of an internationalist set of norms, fails to look behind at an old threat looming from the rear. In fact, Europe's determination to drive on to utopia is so myopic that it actively hinders those nations (Muslim and non-Muslim) that attempt to take effective steps to dampen Islamic radicalism. The United States is left to lead the effort to confront global Jihad both by historical circumstances and the insistence of the jihadists. Jihad is being waged against the U.S., not by a choice America made, but, because the United States is viewed as the remaining obstacle, following the defeat of the Soviet Union, to global Islamization.

The U.S., and especially Europe, are culturally, legally, and militarily ill-prepared to confront the threat. In fact, until 9/11, the leadership of the U.S. did not realize that it was in a Jihad, and Europe still refuses to reach that conclusion. As Islam faces modernity there is a race ongoing to see which response will prevail. Either Islam will reform to come to terms with the twenty-first century, as did Turkey with the demise of the Ottoman Empire in the twentieth century, or it will retreat to the eighth century. Those who believe "Islam is the answer" want an eighth-century world. These voices are currently in the ascendancy and represent the dynamism of the Islamic resurgence. The far fainter voice is of those who wish to reconcile Islam and modernity, and thus reform Islam. Ataturk brought modernity to Turkey by eliminating the dominance of Islam and choosing to emulate Europe through force of personality and arms. Even in that country today, his legacy is being challenged, with broad public support, by an Islamic government. Before Islam can be reformed, however, Muslims must recognize that an Islam that has not adapted to modernity is the problem, not the solution. The U.S. has a great stake in the outcome of this race, as it will determine the length and severity of the Jihad in which the U.S. is engaged.

The failure of the U.S. to recognize, as early as the fall of the Shah in 1979, the consequences of the perception of U.S. weakness in the eyes of the Muslims, was a large contributing factor in the willingness of many Muslims to support an anti-U.S. Jihad. This is an ongoing failure of U.S. strategic intelligence analysis, impacted by years of attention to operational/tactical issues, counterterrorist support, and a cultural divide between the IC and law enforcement communities. The U.S. is still viewing local events in isolation, not as they impact the counter-Jihad — a counter-Jihad that many in the U.S. still refuse to admit we are fighting. It is far easier to treat the symptom, terrorism, than the disease, Islamic Jihad.

America is at long-term risk. It must take decisive action to counter jihadists, but must do so in a way that will not provide them with any sense of victory. Counter-Jihad must be viewed as a whole, and Jihad must be defeated in all its parts. Al-Qa'ida is only a part of the problem. Everywhere that Jihad is declared it must be defeated, and new opportunities must be denied it. Local Jihads in Algeria, Kashmir, Chechnya, the Balkans, Central Asia, Indonesia/Malaysia/Philippines, and Israel/Palestine, must be eliminated. A growing succession of jihadist defeats, not just lengthening the list of Al-Qa'ida killed and captured, is necessary to demonstrate to the Muslim world that the tide has turned against Jihad and its continuance is futile. Only then can the faint voices of Islamic reform and accommodation with modernity be amplified within the dar al-Islam. Until then, not of its own choosing, the U.S. will lead the dar al-Harb. The IC must be made capable, then must persuasively identify, appropriate strategic to tactical opportunities to counter this Jihad.

This is an existential battle for America, more emphatically so than was the Cold War against communism, whose flawed political and economic system collapsed under its own weight. Islam is a religion, a set of beliefs, and fully capable of continuing to motivate its adherents. The task is to motivate Muslims toward the future, as Philip K. Hitti eloquently recommended [see footnote 2 above], and not toward a past of confrontation and violence.

BIBLIOGRAPHY

Abualrub, Jalal. *Holy War Crusades Jihad: In the Torah, the Gospels, and the Quran.* Ed. Alaa Mencke. Orlando: Madinah Publishers and Distributors, 2002.

Ali, Abdullah Yusuf. *The Meaning of the Holy Qur'an.* 9th ed. Beltsville, MD: Amana Publications, 1998.

Al-Sayyid, Mustapha Kamel. "The Other Face of the Islamist Movement." Working Papers, *Carnegie Endowment for International Peace*, Global Policy Program, Democracy and Rule of Law Project, no. 33 (16 January 2003).

Al-Sharq al-Awsat (daily Arabic newspaper), London, 2 Jan 03.

"Arabs Ignore Bin Laden War Call." *Washington Times*, online ed., 13 February 2003. URL: <http://www.washingtontimes.com>. Accessed 13 February 2003.

"Australian Terror Suspect No Longer Facing Charges." *Hong Kong AFP*, online ed., in English, 3 June 2003. URL: <https://datawarehouse10.dia.ic.gov/fcgi-bin/webisdoc?DOC72D+303459+00000b72+repbrag>. Accessed 03 June 2003.

Behrend, Tim. "The Public Teachings of Abu Bakar Ba'asyir." *Ambon PosKo Zwolle,* online ed., in English, 26 May 2003. URL: <https://datawarehouse10.dia.ic.gov/fcgi-bin/webisdoc>. Accessed on Intelink 29 May 2003.

Beschloss, Michael. *The Conquerors: Roosevelt, Truman and the Destruction of Hitler's Germany, 1941-1945.* New York: Simon and Schuster, 2002.

Bird, Steve. "Muslim Cleric is Jailed for Urging Followers to Kill." *The Times* (London), online ed., in English, 8 Mar 2003. URL: <https://datawarehouse10. dia.ic.gov/cgi-bin/webisprt?0000098e+M4+repbrag>. Accessed on Intelink 10 March 2003.

Bodansky, Yossef. "Osama Bin Ladin and the New Crusader War: Bin Laden's New Secret Message to the Islamist Leadership." *Defense and Foreign Affairs Daily*, online ed., 20 February 2003. URL: http://www.StrategicStudies.org.

Busse, Heribert. *Islam, Judaism, and Christianity.* Trans. Allison Brown. Princeton, NJ: Markus Weiner Publishers, 1998.

Chalk, Frank and Kurt Jonassohn. *A History and Sociology of Genocide.* New Haven, CT: Yale University Press, 1990.

Friscolanti, Michael. "Judge Sorry for Delay in Terror Suspect's Case; Held 20 Months: Compares refugee to Prisoners at Guantanamo Bay." *Toronto National Post,* online ed., 12 April 2003. URL: <https://datawarehouse10.dia.ic.gov/cgi-bin/ webisprt?00000a72+M4+repbrag>. Accessed 17 April 2003.

Frye, Richard N. *The Heritage of Central Asia: From Antiquity to Turkish Expansion.* Princeton, NJ: Markus Wiener Publishers, 2001.

Goldziher, Ignaz. *Introduction to Islamic Theology and Law.* Trans. Andras and Ruth Hamori. Princeton, NJ: Princeton University Press, 1981.

Hatcher, William S. and J. Douglass Martin. *The Baha'I Faith: The Emerging Global Religion.* San Francisco: Harper and Row, Publishers, 1984.

Hitti, Philip K. *History of the Arabs: From the Earliest Times to the Present.* 9th ed. New York: St Martin's Press, 1968.

Khadduri, Majid. *War and Peace in the Law of Islam.* Baltimore: The Johns Hopkins Press, 1955.

Knapp, Michael G. "The Concept and Practice of Jihad in Islam." *Parameters* 33, no. 1 (Spring 2003): 82-94.

Kramer, Martin. *Ivory Towers on Sand.* Washington DC: The Washington Institute for Near East Policy, 2001.

"Kurd Mullah Krekar Expelled." *Rotterdam NRC Handelsblad,* online ed., in Dutch, 14 January 2003. URL: <*https://datawarehouse10.dia.ic.gov/cgi-bin/webisprt?00000ab2+M4+dibrarb*>. Accessed 14 January 2003.

Lewis, Bernard. *The Arabs in History.* 6th ed. New York: Oxford University Press.

_____. *The Assassins: A Radical Sect in Islam.* Paperback ed. New York: Basic Books, 2003.

_____. *The Crisis of Islam.* New York: The Modern Library, 2003.

_____. *Cultures in Conflict.* New York: Oxford University Press, 1995.

_____. *Islam and the West.* New York: Oxford University Press, 1993.

_____. *Islam in History.* 2nd ed. Chicago: Open Court Publishing Company, 2001.

_____. *The Multiple Identities of the Middle East.* New York: Schocken Books, 1998.

_____. *The Political Language of Islam.* Chicago: The University of Chicago Press, 1988.

_____. "The Roots of Muslim Rage." *The Atlantic* 266, no 3 (September 1990). URL: <*http://www.theatlantic.com/issues/90sep/rage.htm*>. Accessed 19 December 2002.

_____. *What Went Wrong.* New York: Oxford University Press, 2002.

"London-Based Egyptian Fundamentalist Views Revocation of UK Citizenship." *London Al-Sharq al-Awsat,* online ed., 6 April 2003. URL: <*https://datawarehouse10.dia.ic.gov/cgi-bin/webisprt?00000a4a+M4+repbrag*>. Accessed 07 April 2003.

"Mauritanian Government Arrests Islamic Militants for Alleged Coup Plotting." *Paris AFP World Service,* online ed., in English, 4 June 2003. URL: <*https://datawarehouse10.dia.ic.gov/fcgi-bin/webisdoc? DOC72D+316398+00000b7+repbrag*>. Accessed on Intelink 04 June 2003.

"Netherlands Prosecutor Urges Legal Changes to Improve Fight Against Terrorism." *Rotterdam NRC Handelsblad,* online ed., in Dutch, 19 May 2003. URL: <*https://datawarehouse10.dia.ic.gov/fcgi-bin/webisdoc?DOC72D+169663+00000b32+repbrag*>. Accessed on Intelink 21 May 2003.

"No Arrest Warrant Against German Islamist." *Munich Focus Online,* online ed., in German, 9 May 2003. URL: <*https://datawarehouse10.dia.ic.gov/fcgi-bin/webisdoc?DOC72D+59061+00000b02+repbrag*>. Accessed on Intelink 12 May 2003.

"Norwegian Police Want to Question Iraqi Kurd Suspect." *Paris AFP North European Service,* online ed., in English, 14 Jan 2003. URL: <*https://*

datawarehouse10.dia.ic.gov/cgi-bin/webisprt?00000a36+M4+dibrarb>. Accessed on Intelink 15 January 2003.

Pipes, Daniel. "Wasted Money." *New York Post,* online Edition, 24 June 2003. URL: *<http//www.nypost.com/cgi-bin/printfriendly.pl>*. Accessed 24 June 2003.

"Russian Prosecutors Say Muslim Council May Be Disbanded for Jihad Against U.S." *Moscow Interfax*, online ed., in English, CEP20030404000119 0947 GMT, 4 April 2003. Accessed on Intelink 4 April 2003.

Said, Edward W. *Orientalism.* New York: Pantheon Books, 1978.

"Saudi Arabia: Paper Urged Confrontation of Terrorism." *London Al-Sharq Al Awsat*, GMP20030518000127 0127 GMT, 18 May 2003. Accessed on Intelink 20 May 2003.

"Saudi Muslim Figure Cited on Saudi Scholar's Statement Condemning Riyadh Bombing." On *Doha Al-Jazirah*, Satellite Channel Television in Arabic. Doha Al-Jazirah airdate 19 May 2003, GMP20030520000039, 2025 GMT. Accessed on Intelink 20 May 2003.

"Trial of 12 'Suspected Muslim Extremists' Opens in Rotterdam 12 May." *Paris AFP, North European Service*, online ed., in English, 12 May 2003. URL: *<https://datawarehouse10.dia.ic.gov/fcgi-bin/webisdoc?DOC72D+76795+00000b02+repbrag>*. Accessed on Intelink 12 May 2003.

"We Have Voided the Bases of Bin-Ladin's Fetwas." *London Al-Majallah*, in Arabic, 23 February 2003 through 02 March 2003.

"Writer Criticizes Al-Azhar's 'Strange' Fatwa on Acquiring Foreign Citizenship." *London Al-Sharq al-Awsat*, online ed., in Arabic, 17 March 2003. URL: *<https://datawarehouse10.dia.ic.gov/cgi-bin/webisprt?000009ce+M4+repbrag>*. Accessed on Intelink 18 March 2003.

ABOUT THE AUTHOR

The author has been a U.S. Government employee for more than 30 years. He was a Soviet Foreign Area Specialist with the U.S. Army and subsequently a DIA analyst of Soviet policy in the Middle East. He holds BA and MA degrees in International Relations and is a graduate of the U.S. Army Russian Institute, the Defense Language Institute (Russian), Army Foreign Area Officer's course (Africa) and Army Command and General Staff College. He served as the Deputy Director of the Middle East Seminar at the Army School of International Studies and has been a full-time member of the JMIC faculty, having held a chair in Intelligence Analysis and Production. He remains on the adjunct faculty of the College and continues to work in a national intelligence agency.

www.ingramcontent.com/pod-product-compliance
Lightning Source LLC
Chambersburg PA
CBHW081551280526

45788CB00011B/3441